Strategic Comm

MW00778427

Strategic Communication comprises different forms of goal-oriented communication inside and between organizations, their stakeholders and the society. Strategic communication is an emerging practice and research field integrating established disciplines such as public relations, organizational communication and marketing communication into a holistic framework. The field is based on an awareness of the fundamental importance of communication for the existence and performance of all organizations.

This textbook offers a broad insight into the field of strategic communication. The main aim of the book is to give a general overview of theories, concepts and methods in strategic communication. The book also aims to develop an understanding of different perspectives and the consequences each one has for practice. After reading the book the student or reader will be able to define and reflect upon strategic communication as an academic field and professional practice, describe relevant theories and apply these to communication problems.

The authors apply a reflective and practice-oriented approach meaning earlier research or theories are not only described, but also discussed from different critical perspectives. A practice-oriented approach means, in this book, that the authors strongly emphasize the role of contexts and situations—where strategic communication actually happens. This book will help business and communications students to not only define and understand a variety of strategic communications theories, but to use those theories to generate communication strategy and solutions.

Jesper Falkheimer and **Mats Heide** are professors in Strategic Communication at the Department of Strategic Communication, Lund University in Sweden.

Strategic Communication
An introduction

Jesper Falkheimer and Mats Heide

Routledge
Taylor & Francis Group

LONDON AND NEW YORK

First published 2018
by Routledge
2 Park Square, Milton Park, Abingdon, Oxon OX14 4RN

and by Routledge
711 Third Avenue, New York, NY 10017

Routledge is an imprint of the Taylor & Francis Group, an informa business

© 2018 Jesper Falkheimer and Mats Heide

British Library Cataloguing in Publication Data
A catalogue record for this book is available from the British Library

Library of Congress Cataloging in Publication Data
Names: Falkheimer, Jesper, author. | Heide, Mats, author.
Title: Strategic communication : an introduction / Jesper Falkheimer and Mats Heide.
Description: Abingdon, Oxon ; New York, NY : Routledge, 2018. |
Includes bibliographical references and index. |
Identifiers: LCCN 2017050232 (print) | LCCN 2017053492 (ebook) |
 ISBN 9781315621555 (eBook) | ISBN 9781138657045 (hardback : alk. paper) | ISBN 9781138657038 (pbk. : alk. paper)
Subjects: LCSH: Communication in organizations. | Communication in management.
Classification: LCC HD30.3 (ebook) | LCC HD30.3 .F35 2018 (print) |
 DDC 658.4/5–dc23
LC record available at https://lccn.loc.gov/2017050232

ISBN: 9781138657045 (hbk)
ISBN: 9781138657038 (pbk)
ISBN: 9781315621555 (ebk)

Typeset in Garamond
by Taylor & Francis Books

Contents

List of illustrations

Figures

Tables

Boxes

Preface

This fundamental textbook is the first that covers the quickly expanding and popular field of strategic communication. Strategic communication is a multi-disciplinary subject, relevant to several sectors of late modern society—in business, government, politics and culture. The main aim of the book is to give undergraduate students a general overview of theories, concepts and methods in strategic communication. The book also aims to develop an understanding of different perspectives and the consequences they have for strategic communication in theory and practice. After reading the book the reader will be able to define and reflect upon strategic communication as an academic field and professional practice, describe relevant theories and apply these to communication problems.

Strategic communication is *the purposeful use of communication by an organization to fulfill its mission* (Hallahan, Holtzhausen, van Ruler, Verčič, & Sriramesh, 2007). From a historical perspective, strategic communication is as old as organizations, since organizations *per se* always have goals and are communicative. But from a managerial and professional angle strategic communication has a shorter history. From a research perspective, strategic communication is an emerging field of knowledge bridging established research fields such as public relations, organizational communication, and marketing communications. In the broadest sense of the term, organization in this context refers to private companies, public authorities and organizations, associations, and interest and activist groups. During the last two decades, strategic communication has become institutionalized in the international academic community through university departments, educational programs, professorships, scientific journals, handbooks, conferences, and so forth. Tench, Verhoeven and Zerfaß (2009) concluded that strategic communication is institutionalized in two different ways: (a) as a behavioral organizational pattern and (b) as a cognitive managerial perspective, meaning that strategic communication has become a critical aspect integrated in decision-making and planning. This conclusion is based on a European survey and not valid for all parts of the world, but with less doubt in most developed countries. This textbook explains core concepts and theories in strategic communication, using examples from earlier research and our experience from practice. We begin by explaining fundamental concepts about communication, organization, and strategy, then go on to explore some crucial communication processes such as leadership, social change, mediatization, crisis, and change. Finally, we make some reflections on the current status of the field of strategic communication and discuss some new approaches and concepts such as "the communicative organization."

The value of strategic communication

Later in the book we will go into different definitions of our subject, but here we start the other way around and describe three contemporary situations where strategic communication is practiced.

First, imagine yourself as a manager and member of the executive committee in a corporation selling mobile phones. One day a regional manager calls you and says: We have a problem. The same day a human rights group has started a campaign against your corporation due to the fact that an investigatory report has shown that the mobile phones are produced by a subcontractor in a South Asian country by workers who are treated badly by their superior staff. There are documented examples of workers who have protested towards the working conditions being physical punished. As you speak, hundreds of customers and non-customers are posting critical messages on the corporation's social media channels. News media journalists are starting to call managers and employees trying to get comments. Employees are wondering what is going on; several are ashamed of their corporation. The main issue here is not a communication issue; rather it is a question of working conditions, organizational control, ethics, and sustainability. But it is also a typical situation where theories and practices of strategic communication are called for. The corporation stands in front of several strategic communication questions: How do we handle the flood of critique in the social media channels? What do we answer the journalists? Who will be the spokesperson? How do we reach out to the over 10 000 employees situated in twelve different countries? How do we communicate with the other different stakeholder groups such as customers, investors, government and politicians? Can we base our activities in any strategy or plan? Our corporate brand is well ranked by the customers according to the latest measurement—what will happen now and how may we repair our image? These are all typical strategic communication questions, involving the whole organization and transgressing borders between actions and communications, developed in an organizational crisis.

A second example, aiming to increase understanding of the relevance and value of strategic communication, involves issues of trust and democracy in society. Imagine yourself as a communications officer working for the national police authority. According to a national survey answered by a representative sample of citizens in your country, public trust in the police has decreased by 20 percent since last year. There may be several reasons for this: a decline in solved crimes, internal dissatisfaction with a reorganization within the police that led to a public debate, or a recent investigative TV documentary that questioned police efficiency and management. All organizations depend on trust among their internal and external stakeholders and this is even more true for judicial and security authorities. The main reasons behind the decline in organizational trust may be facts rather than communicative issues, but even if that is the case, there is always a strategic communicative dimension. In the case used here, it may be that the reorganization in itself is questionable, leading to a decline in solved crimes and public questioning of police efficiency. But it is also possible that there are communication problems that need to be addressed. Perhaps the organizational change process has failed due to a bad implementation of the new organization. If the police management has not been able to break down and communicate the new strategy so that it is interpreted as meaningful for employees, it is a matter of communication failure, which leads to a decline in efficiency. The negative discussion that occurred outside the organization, where journalists have reproduced internal criticism, may be a consequence of this. As a communication officer, you have several challenges to handle. You must of course manage the direct adverse situation and support and advise managers with facts, information, messages, and channels. Even more important is to systematically listen to internal and external stakeholders and develop a plan for how to regain organizational trust.

A third example showing the relevance and value of strategic communication is public diplomacy. The concept of public diplomacy is debated among scholars. From a traditional standpoint, public diplomacy is strategic communication from a nation-state to publics in other countries aiming to influence them and promoting national interests, especially regarding foreign policy. Since the millennium shift, several scholars have challenged this traditional sender-oriented approach and the concept of *new* public diplomacy has emerged (Pamment, 2013). New public diplomacy involves not only national states but also non-state organizations. The role of global media technology is crucial to the development of new public diplomacy, based on a more complex and interactive view of communication (Leonardi & Bailey, 2008). Imagine yourself as a communications consultant hired by the department of defense in your country. After signing several confidentiality agreements, you are invited to be a member of a communications team that has the task of countering disinformation spread by a foreign power through social and traditional media in different parts of the world. Media analysis and opinion polls show that your country is becoming increasingly associated with national insecurity, political extremism, and violence in the streets. The negative image has begun to have negative consequences such as reduced tourism, a decline in foreign investments, and problems with international cooperation. Facts and figures show that the negative images that are spread about your country are based on rumors and disinformation deliberately spread by a foreign power to harm your country's national interests. The communications team has to analyze the situation, create a communication strategy, and enforce this through various activities. The task is extremely demanding since you need to both oppose the spread of disinformation and re-establish an accurate image of your country. You cannot use unethical methods and must be aware that a counter campaign may increase polarization and amplification.

All three examples show that strategic communication, viewed as a practical toolbox filled with persuasion strategies and tactics, is a double-edged sword. As with social media, for example (Smudde, 2005), these strategies and tactics may be used for something good, but may also be used for manipulation and propaganda. Just as much as democratic states, corporations and NGOs, terrorism organizations also implement and use strategic communication strategies and tactics.

The approach and structure

This textbook aims to give a broad insight into the field of strategic communication, but obviously, we as authors have a perspective that influences the structure and content. In simplified terms, we apply a reflective and practice-oriented approach. A *reflective approach* means that we not only describe earlier research or theories but also discuss them from different critical perspectives. A *practice-oriented approach* means, in this book, that we strongly emphasize the role of contexts and situations—where communication happens. This does not necessarily mean that we reject all general models, but we are skeptical towards universal claims when it comes to strategic communication.

There is often a large discrepancy between what is discussed and debated at the forefront of research and what is discussed in class. Czarniawska (2008) discusses the same problem in the field of business administration. According to Czarniawska, teaching is often based on traditional theories that are normative; they point towards a desired direction and a desired position. Such theories are usually easy to visualize in general models. Czarniawska believes that simple models have an attraction, not necessarily due to their actual explanatory power but due to their aesthetic appeal. Complex phenomena are simplified into decontextualized models. This is the reason why we see simplified communication models reproduced and used in textbooks, especially in the management and marketing fields. The simple and rhetorically powerful models are thus used in basic training, and practitioners who have learned these theories have them as a starting point and reference point (see Varey, 2000). This is problematic because many managers emerge from a university education colored by a certain, simple approach to communication that is linked to linearity, fixed communications roles (transmitter and receiver), and causality (have an uni-directional effect). In this book, we do not present one easy solution or model, how rhetorically convincing this might be. Our ambition is to reduce the discrepancy between recent research and textbooks. We also believe that students of strategic communication need to get an insight into the whole picture of the field: the history, theories, and methods. This is what this book aims to give the reader, but we strongly encourage serious students (and practitioners) to dig deeper and also read original texts. In this book we use as many references as we can and we hope that the curious reader will look at these too.

The structure of the book is, hopefully, easy to grasp. Here we briefly describe the different parts. *The introduction* describes the evolution of strategic communication in modern organizations and society. We will define the field, reflect upon the concept, and contextualize strategic communication. In a simple and clear way we will make the case for developing deeper knowledge about strategic communication from societal, organizational and critical perspectives. The concept of reflexivity will be used in a discussion about the intimate relationship between communication and organizations. In the second part, we will describe the development of practice and highlight some of the main industry trends, issues, and challenges (with a specific focus on digitalization and its consequences). After the introduction, we have divided the book into two main sections: *fundamentals* (what is communication; what is strategy—and strategic communication?) and *communication processes* (focusing on different communication processes that are related to society and organizations).

In the first fundamental chapter, *What is communication?*, we define communication and present a selection of communication theories relevant to the management of communication within and between organizations and society. Communication and related concepts such as information and sensemaking are discussed. Two basic perspectives are defined: communication as transmission or as ritual. Then a number of key theories of communication are presented, e.g. rhetoric, transmission models (from 1920 onwards), and persuasion models (e.g. agenda-setting theory and dissonance theory), critical communication theory (Habermas's theory of communicative and strategic action), as well as normative and instrumental models (e.g. the Excellence study). In the second part of the chapter we focus on contemporary theories of co-creation and digital communication. We describe communication theory from a historical perspective, stressing that its development should be seen as a dialectic movement that oscillates between the transmission and sensemaking ideals.

In the second fundamental chapter, *What is strategy?*, the aims are to discuss and reflect on how the concept of strategy may be interpreted from a communication perspective and to develop arguments for an increased emphasis on a practice- and process-oriented approach. Initially, we describe how traditional strategy theory is built on a philosophy of rationality. Examples are given of how organization executives and their advisors construct goal-oriented plans, which are implemented through different tactics at different and lower levels in the organizations. These strategies are expected to be based on valid and relevant background research; there are several methods for obtaining background material in strategic communication such as benchmark analysis, media analysis, and quantitative surveys focusing attitudes towards an issue or phenomenon. The four stages for optimizing communication are described:

research, planning, implementation, and evaluation. In the second half of the chapter we reflect upon the traditional strategy approach, link this to the transmission model of communication, and develop arguments for an increased emphasis on a practice- and process-oriented approach. Four strategy perspectives (classical, evolutionary, processual, and systemic) developed by Whittington (2001) are analyzed and linked to strategic communication. The processual perspective is developed further, focusing what practitioners actually do when they act as communication strategists in organizations.

In the last fundamental chapter, *What is strategic communication?*, we integrate theories and ideas from the earlier chapters and deepen the discussion about strategic communication that was begun in the introduction. Initially, we describe the history and main theories in the three interrelated fields that are integrated in strategic communication: public relations, organizational communication, and marketing communication (with an emphasis on branding). We then present examples of attempts to integrate these fields and discuss concepts such as corporate communication, integrated communication, and communication management. The relationships between different communication logics in marketing and strategic communication are analyzed. In the main part of the chapter we present strategic communication as a field of knowledge (definitions, models, etc.). We also give an insight into practitioners' roles and perspectives and list relevant journals, business sources, and so forth that students may use to gain deeper knowledge.

In the next section we focus on different and crucial strategic communication processes.

First, we present broad theories and ideas about *society, social change, and strategic communication*. In this introductory chapter, the aim is to give a broad overview of strategic communication from a societal perspective. We discuss modernity, postmodernity, and late modernity from different angles. We conclude that the established disciplines public relations, marketing communications, and organizational communication can be interpreted as linked to the modern mass society that developed during the last centuries, while strategic communication may be viewed as a consequence of late modernity. The chapter links back to the introduction in so far as it increases the understanding of why strategic communication has evolved to become a powerful practice in society.

Second, we focus on *organizational identity and culture*, which constitute the foundation of an organization. Organizational identity is produced and reproduced by communication and should never be understood as completed or fixed. Often, organizational identity is understood as a social process when members identify themselves with an organization. This identification and what organizational members see as important values of an organization depends on background, interest, profession, and so forth. Hence, there are often several different identities within a single organization. Organizational culture encompasses among other things values, norms, beliefs, habits, and principles among organizational members. As is the case with organizational

identities there are often several cultures within an organization. Organizational culture is also a product of communication and is consolidated by
continuous communication processes. In this chapter we will present both the
traditional understanding of these two phenomena and contrast it with new,
alternative research that questions the possibility of controlling and managing
organizational members when it comes to organizational identity and culture.
We focus on *communicative leadership and coworkership:* two processes that have
excited considerable interest among both practitioners and scholars. Leadership is one of most researched fields within the research fields of management,
psychology, and organizational communication. Even if organizational identity
and culture are prerequisites for a well-functioning organization and also the
most effective forms of control, it would not be possible for an organization to
survive in the long run without both leadership and coworkership. The
important role of communication in the leadership process has been
acknowledged since the 1930s. Communication is a large part of leadership.
Modern research emphasizes that leadership is a dual process, enacted by both
the leader and coworkers (or followers as they are more commonly termed in the
literature). The fundamental role of coworkers and coworkership in organizations
has recently become widely accepted.

Third, we discuss *change and crisis communication*, two of the most important
fields and disciplines for communication professionals. Scholars have for decades declared that we live in a postmodern, liquid, fluid, and ever-changing
risk society, and this has certain consequences for organizations. There are
many risks, internal and external, that might evolve into a crisis. Today this is
very common, with large organizational change processes aiming to adapt to
changes in the market, new technological innovations, or just because there is
a strong managerial discourse that proclaim change programs. There are many
similarities between change processes and crisis situations. Both produce
increased uncertainty and create a significant need for information, communication, and sensemaking. We will present and discuss both traditional and
contemporary research within these two fields.

Fourth, we highlight *mediatization: from traditional to social media.* The role
of traditional news media and social media is highlighted in this chapter. The
aim is to review the literature on news media, social media, and strategic
communication, describing the new communication structure, and challenge
old concepts and perspectives. The chapter discusses the role of news media
and media relations but mainly focuses on social media as technologies woven
into a social and cultural communication structure. Participatory communication strategies are presented, as well as theories of propaganda in old and
new contexts. The chapter addresses some of the challenges, opportunities,
threats, and changed practices that can arise from an organization's approach
to participatory communication through use of social media. Different examples
are used to illustrate the pros and cons of social media: how corporations can
create new forms of communication processes and how terrorist movements
can use social media for unethical strategic communications.

In the final part, *future developments*, we present our ideas for future development within the field. This is executed by using the emerging concept of the communicative organization. In this chapter we focus on contemporary trends and the latest research about strategic communication from an organizational approach.

The target group of this book is primarily undergraduate students in strategic communication, which may be the core of a whole education program or a course in a program with another core discipline such as business administration, political science, journalism, or basically any other field (since strategic communication is valid as a dimension in most fields). We also direct the book towards practitioners in communications, management, marketing, and so forth who want to develop their thinking and doing.

We want to thank our colleagues and students at the Department of Strategic Communication at Lund University, Sweden as well as all our international colleagues for giving us continuous inspiration. We also want to thank all the clever and reflective communication professionals who have developed our thinking.

Jesper Falkheimer and Mats Heide
January 2018

Introduction

Strategic communication is a knowledge field and interest within several academic subjects. Consequently, theories and knowledge in strategic communication originate from several adjacent disciplines. From a traditional perspective, there are two fundamental approaches for practitioners and researchers. One is an organizational approach that focuses on the importance of strategic communication processes for organizational efficiency, culture, democracy, management, and similar aspects. The other is a societal approach where the strategic communication processes are analyzed from the attitudes or behavior of the public, the formation of public opinion, democracy, culture, and so forth. We believe that both approaches are important and valuable, and that they are mutually beneficial. These approaches provide practitioners and researchers with better opportunities to understand the complex organizational life and the role of communication. As such, the ideal is to produce a creative and critical double vision that takes us further towards a holistic perspective that is a core characteristic of strategic communication.

We understand strategic communication to be the conscious organizational communication efforts to reach the overall goals (Falkheimer & Heide, 2011a). In the center stands not the goals of a certain communication effort or project, but the work-related long-term goals or organizational mission (Frandsen & Johansen, 2017). Strategic communication is based on an awareness of the fundamental importance of communication for the existence and performance of an organization. Hence, communication is not only a tool for information dissemination or conversations between people.

The purpose of this introduction is to put strategic communication in a context and to demonstrate show its importance in contemporary organizations. In Chapter 3 we will go deeper into a discussion of strategic communication, integrating the discussion of communication in Chapter 1 and the reasoning of strategy in Chapter 2.

Reflexivity

In this book we advocate a reflexive approach. That implies a critical understanding of on the one hand acting and thinking and on the other the framework of interpretation (which chiefly consists of academic theories, private theories, and experiences), norms, and values. The mainstream literature on strategic communication, public relations, and corporate communication builds on a "being-realism" ontology (see Chia, 1996) that celebrates rationalism and representationalism. We have written about the need for an alternative to the dominating managerial perspective within these fields (Falkheimer & Heide, 2016). Other researchers—for example, David McKie (2001)—state that the field of public relations is too insular and "cannot stick with the traditional 'value-free and neutral scientific observations' [...] of old research paradigms" (p. 91). However, there are now signs of an increasing interest among researchers in alternative perspectives, e.g. L'Etang (2004a), Ihlen and Verhoeven (2012), and Christensen and Cornelissen (2011). It is even possible to talk of a "reflexive turn" characterizing researchers who are aware of and discuss the active role they have in constructing a social reality when performing research. Both the collection of empirical material and the reporting is a construction process in which certain aspects of the reality are chosen, analyzed through certain theories, and finally reported in articles, book chapters, and books. Hence, the reflexive turn stands in sharp contrast to the still dominant belief that researchers are neutral and completely objective.

To reflect is a question of meta-thinking—that is, thinking about thinking or interpretations of interpretations (Alvesson, 2003). A reflective approach is a prerequisite of learning and development. It is first when we leave our ingrained opinions and perfunctory line of thought that we can see and understand new things, and consequently generate new knowledge, which can be used to develop practice. A very good example on reflexivity is Mats Alvesson and Andrew Spicer's (2012) article *A stupidity-based theory of organizations*, which has received a lot of attention in media, even outside the ordinary academic circle of readers. According to the authors, *"functional stupidity"* is a lack of reflexivity and refusal to use the intellectual capacity in an organization. Alvesson and Spicer oppose the common starting point that organizations become successful through mobilizing the cognitive capacity that is collected to management and coworkers. In a short sight, functional stupidity can—when organizational members for instance do not question different ways to performing a task—even be good since it makes the organization focused and action oriented. Nevertheless, functional stupidity has obviously also negative aspects, such as unmotivated, cynical, and negative coworkers, and it can even have negative consequences in the long run from both an organizational and societal perspective. The interesting with the approach that Alvesson and Spice take is that it goes beyond the normal frames and attentions something that rarely is discussed and often taken for granted.

A prerequisite for a reflexive approach is a willingness to learn new things. And a reflexive approach is also an absolute condition for becoming a more professional practitioner (Schön, 1983). Further, there is also a need for some form of tool that can help a person reflect. Such tools are offered in this book.

Theories are tools that help us see and understand the surrounding "reality," and different kinds of theory guide what we focus on, perceive, and understand. Consequently, we see theories as lenses through which we consider the "reality". This perception of theories stands in contrast to the traditional and positivistic understanding of theories as "true" descriptions of the reality. Later in the book we will dig deeper into philosophy of science questions concerning what can be regarded as knowledge and reality.

There is a widespread notion that a clear border exists between theory and practice, that theory and research, which only researchers deal with, are divorced from reality. You may find this notion in several different contexts and we have been amazed at all the instances that reproduce this understanding. Theory is often regarded as something meaningless and complicated that does not add something real or useful. However, this is not so. We—as researchers—would instead underline that strategic communication rather suffers from the opposite: there are too few theories and there is a need for more research in the field. More research is needed partly to develop the aggregated knowledge in strategic communication and partly because the practice needs to be refined, examined, and developed. For example, much research shows that the large marketing campaigns we constantly face are rarely efficient—at least not in the long run. Nevertheless, new campaigns of this kind are constantly carried out. Could this be explained by the fact that marketers and advertising agencies lack tools to perform other forms of communication?

One explanation of the negative perception of theorizing as something that burdens and departs from reality has its basis in the current view of knowledge. According to this view, knowledge is the product of work by researchers who, with the help of quantitative methods, have captured objective and true pictures of the reality "out there." Knowledge is then understood as a true mirror of reality. This has a strong relation to communication and language. Traditionally, language is also perceived as a mirror, based on the belief that it is possible to communicate a "true" picture of objective reality through language.

In a late modern view of knowledge there is an emphasis on the close relationship between theory and practice: one cannot exist without the other, they are mutually dependent. From this perspective, knowledge is understood as a perspective—a particular understanding of a phenomenon. Language is regarded as a tool with which we produce our own understanding. Hence, there is no objective reality, only a subjective reality for each human being, created together with other humans with the help of communication. In other words, knowledge is relative and contextual. The metaphor that is used for knowledge in this context is glasses or lenses. By using different glasses, we can obtain different understandings and knowledge. With this view of knowledge there follows an understanding that knowledge and knowledge development is closely related to action and practice. Theories are by no means highfalutin, a departure from "reality." In an earlier book (in Swedish),

Reflexive Communication (2003), we underlined that all communication professionals are theorists. Every single communication professional uses abstraction and inference to explain or understand how things are connected, and they use their own theories and models to solve problems.

We maintain that the collaboration between researchers and practitioners is fundamentally important and we therefore welcome all initiatives that try to reduce the gap between research and practice. This was the reason we invited practitioners to write texts in our anthology *Strategic Communication: Research and practice* (in Swedish) (2011). The development of this cooperation makes only slow progress—far too slow. A larger and more frequent exchange of knowledge, thoughts, and ideas between practitioners and researchers would be very rewarding for all parties. We would also like to see greater interest, by both parties, in each others' activities and contributions.

A close relation

Researchers long ago pointed out the close relation between communication and organizations. Already in 1938 the American business executive Chester Barnard, who summarized his successful career in the widely distributed *The Functions of the Executive* (1938/1968), emphasized that communication is a fundamental part of an organization and that leadership and communication are closely related. However, it was the publication of the second edition of the American organizational psychologist Karl E. Weick's (1979) now classic text *The Social Psychology of Organizing* that prompted researchers in organization studies to start paying serious attention to the central importance that communication has in the continuous organizing process. The view of organizations that Weick presents in the book stands in glaring contrast to the traditional, slightly static, understanding of organizations. Weick (2004) claims that organizations are made up of a large number of formal and informal interpersonal relations between persons and that these relations must be continually maintained. This occurs through interaction and communication, which "renegotiates"—i.e. improves or weakens—each relationship. In most cases the social structure that makes up an organization—that is, all relationships in an organization that form a pattern—will be reproduced, but the structure can also be changed in some direction. According to Weick, it is communication that produces and reproduces organizations. Communication is a basic element of all organizations and their activities. The daily organizing happens as much through informal dialogues in rooms and corridors as through formal decisions (Czarniawska, 2008). Hence, it is impossible for an organization to exist without communication; an organization without communication will dissolve and cease to exist (Weick, 1995).

The communication of organizations has interested communication professionals and researchers primarily in the fields of public relations and organizational communication. But marketing researchers too have increasingly started to stress the importance of communication for successful marketing activities. From a historical point of view marketing has been product driven, with communication generally treated as secondary. Marketing has now entered a new era, one that can be described as information driven, interactive, and consumer focused, and communication is emphasized for successful marketing campaigns. From the beginning of the twenty-first century integrated marketing communication, a concept that takes a holistic approach to an organization's communication, with effective marketing communication as its the goal (Cornelissen, 2000), has been on the agenda. Another popular concept within marketing is relationship marketing, where communication again is put at the center and relations, networks, and interaction are stressed (Grönroos, 2000; Gummesson, 1995). It is also interesting to notice that a modern definition of marketing (see Kotler, 2016) draws on the classical definition of public relations: to produce good long-term relationships with important publics. Accordingly, there will be other communication requirements between an organization and its customers. Nowadays, different forms of advertising campaign and publicity stunts are not sufficient. Rather, the need is for more long-term and relations-aimed communication.

In other words, an important point of departure for this book is that there is a close relationship between communication and organizations (Heide, Johansson, & Simonsson, 2012; Putnam & Nicotera, 2009). Communication is a requisite for the existence of an organization. It is through formal and informal communication between organizational members and between the organization and its surroundings that an organization is enacted. Conversations and texts produce and reproduce an organization. When organizational members communicate, it generates both their own and others' picture of what constitutes the organization, what the organizational structure looks like, how the communication climate is perceived, what the competitors are and which qualities they have, what organizational threats exist, the future of the organization, and so on. However, it is not only organizational members' communication that is of importance to the production and reproduction of an organization. Those outside the formal organization, who cannot be described as organizational members, are also important for producing the "pictures" and understanding of an organization. Discussions among, for example, citizens, consumers, distributors, stockholders, and stakeholders produce, evolve, and improve pictures and understandings of an organization—that is, a certain image. Especially important contributors to shaping people's view of an organization are journalists and mass media. Very frequently, mass media report what Boorstin (1963/1985) calls *pseudo-events*— that is, events that are put on by organizations with the aim of attracting the attention of the mass media and thereby generating publicity. Examples of pseudo-events are press conferences, press releases, advertising, and interviews with top managers. In addition, journalists themselves act as target-seeking missiles and looking for events that are within the frame of the media logic— in other words, the production of media "tends to be evocative, encapsulated, highly thematic, familiar to audiences, and easy to use" (Altheide, 2004,

p. 294). Often, *media logic* leads to simplification, polarization, intensification, concretization, personalization, and stereotypes. Media logic implies that things that suit the mass media's format, organization, working conditions, and norms have a greater chance of becoming news (Altheide & Snow, 1979). The wide use of social media means that new patterns are being made, but media logic seems to play a part even there.

Summing up, we would like to emphasize that conversations and texts are not objective descriptions or mirror pictures of a certain "truth" or of "reality." Rather, the conversations and texts produce a particular version of reality and truth. We can conclude from this that the talk and texts do something, since they have both social and political consequences (Potter & Wetherell, 1987). How we understand and describe reality—to our selves and to others—influences our thinking and acting.

An increasing interest in communication

International research at Reuters Institute, University of Oxford reveals a steady trend in Western countries, with communication professionals increasing in number and journalists decreasing in number—in contrast to, for example, India. In general, Western organizations spend immense amounts of money on different forms of communication, especially when it comes to external communication. Advertising campaigns, crisis communication, branding activities, communication via social media with different forms of stakeholders—there is a vast list of examples of what organizations do to maintain good and long-term relations with vital stakeholders, increase their status, trust, and reputation, and naturally achieve a return on invested money.

Another trend is that more and more organizational leaders understand and value the importance of communication. They understand that it is communication that drives an organization and that malfunctioning communication has serious negative effects (Falkheimer, Heide, Simonsson, Zerfass, & Verhoeven, 2016). It is now usual for leadership courses to make communication a fundamental part of the education. In traditional leadership courses managers learnt how to become better rhetoricians and make cogent slide presentations, but now there is often greater emphasis on the vital relation between organization and communication. In other words, there is in general a more strategic understanding of the importance of communication for a successful organization.

Although there are many signs that communication is attracting more attention from organizations, it remains a Cinderella subject. Communication is often regarded as something rather simple, at bottom just a matter of disseminating information to different receiver groups. Over and over again the so-called transmission view of communication—that is, communication seen as a linear process between a sender and receivers—predominates. (This view of communication is discussed at length in Chapter 1.)

There are many examples of marketing communication, management communication, crisis communication, and change communication with this traditional understanding of communication. The problem with the transmission model is that its primary focus is the message and finding the most efficient medium for a certain task. What is ignored is the interpretation of the message. A message does not have a fixed meaning; its meaning is produced by the receivers, depending on their background, interests, education, and so forth. Communication is a complex and mutual activity that takes place between all participants in a communication process. This raises the question of whether it is even possible to measure the effects of communication, and consequently whether a communication professional can ever demonstrate the importance of communication within the organization and in wider society. During the 1980s there was a substantial discourse on the value of measuring communication activities and in our experience this question is still significant for many communication professionals (Tench, Verčič, Zerfass, Moreno, & Verhoeven, 2017). Models and formats that could give answers regarding the effects of communication represent the holy grail for communication professionals (Pavlik, 1987). However, the sad truth is that there never has been and probably never will be any simple model that could measure the effects of organizations' communication work and communication activities (Lindenmann, 1993).

Top management and communication

These days there is great demand for managers to be able to communicate complex phenomena such as values, norms, visions and overall goals, organizational identity, and organizational culture to different kinds of receiver both inside and outside the organization. Skill in this area is often crucial in the recruitment of new managers. In other words, strategic communication is no longer confined to communication professionals. Rather, it is something that concerns managers and leaders at all organizational levels. A Danish investigation of managers' relation to and work with communication shows that most top managers put good communication with coworkers at the top of their agenda (Lund & Petersen, 2002). At the same time, our research projects show that this prioritization is not always seen in practice. We are often told that communication issues are not on the management's agenda and that the communication department is perceived as part of organizational headquarters, tasked with disseminating information from management to coworkers and others in order to influence them in a certain direction. When you interview organizational members, you must always reflect on the interviewees' statements and ask *why* they answer as they do. It is also important to consider what they are *not* telling you. It is not always the objective "truth" (if this even exists!) that you receive in an interview. We all want to make a good impression in different situations—we want to show that we have done our homework, know a lot, and follow the debate (Alvesson, 2011). An interview has consequently a large element of *impression management* (Goffman, 1959). Interviews are conversations, situations where a certain social reality is formed and constructed. The managers that Lund and Petersen interviewed in the Danish study, referred to above, would certainly have wanted to show that they were "modern" and knew about the importance of communication for organizations. We draw the conclusion that there is a lot of space for more research on what happens in organizations and how organizational members understand communication.

Brands and communication

How is it possible that people have such formed opinions of different organizations? Why do many feel that Adidas is a cooler and better brand than other manufactures of sneakers such as Puma, Nike, or Reebok? Why do many prefer products from Apple rather than products from Samsung, Microsoft, Asus, or HP. Why do some people think that Alfa Romeo feels more "right" than other car manufacturers such as BMW, Toyota, or Chrysler? These views probably do not reflect preferences based on products' or services' actual advantages or disadvantages. Few of us do a systematic investigation of product reviews before we decide to buy a product. A certain brand just feels the best within a certain product category. But why is it like that?

One answer is that we as consumers have relations to some organizations. If good relations have been developed, there is a better chance that we will behave loyally to the organization when new products or services are offered to us. The relations are to a great extent based on the understanding we have of an organization and its products. These understandings are partly formed by mediated information (the messages that organizations send out via their brands and advertising), partly by media reports about an organization, and partly by our own experience of an organization—for instance, how we are treated by the telephone operator or sales person and how we experience a product. Many understandings are based on the experiences of other people, such as friends, relatives, colleagues, and neighbors. In ordinary, daily conversations people often discuss different organizations and their products and this helps form fairly fixed opinions. In sum, we are not fully rational as individuals and develop our life world and understanding in communication with others (dialogues face to face and different forms of text such as social media and news articles).

Brands are something that modern organizations put a lot of energy and invest a lot of money in. This can partly be explained by today's major international competition—it is much more difficult to copy a brand than a product or service—and partly by a changed attitude among consumers: we often consume in order to improve or change our identity and we are attracted by the values that different manufacturers and organizations offer (e.g. exclusivity, security, or traditionalism).

Coworkers are the most important ambassadors of an organization, and their work and relation-building activities are a fundamental part of an organization's branding. How customers and other stakeholders perceive the staff's helpfulness, knowledge, and competence is much more important for the brand than other forms of communication activity such as adverting. Since the staff is the "face outward" they are of fundamental importance to the success of an organization (White & Park, 2010). Richard Normann (1984) has called the situation when an organization can show what qualities a service has the *moments of truth*. An organization must respond to these moments as well as they possibly can, since after the customer has left it is difficult to add more value to the quality experience. During the 1980s the former CEO of the Scandinavian airline company SAS, Jan Carlzon (1989) emphasized the importance of these moments of truth, when the staff in different situations meet customers. It is critical that staff members make a good impression and start to build a good relationship with the customer.

Services, intangible values and communication

The service sector has during the last decades increasingly expanded and there is a common understanding in many countries today that we have left behind the old, traditional production economy and entered the knowledge and service society (Sveiby, 1994). However, it is not useful to indicate how many service companies there are in the world, since the statistic is stuck in the industrial era's understanding of service. Christian Grönroos (2015), an internationally known marketing researcher, underlines that manufacturing companies also offer services. It is possible to differentiate between revenue-producing service and hidden service. The first category embraces, for example, the service that consultants, banks, insurance companies, hotels, travel agencies, and restaurants offer. The second category consists of more or less invisible service that is part of a product's total cost, such as research and development, quality control, sales, complaints, and reclamation of broken products and recycling of return product such as glass bottles and batteries. This reasoning requires us to accept that all manufactures also offer a quantity of services. With this extended understanding, service becomes something that all organizations offer their customers and stakeholders. Further, Grönroos claims that it is actually not products or services that customers buy, but the *advantages* that these offer us. Services can be understood as the service customers see in an organizational offer and which can produce some form of value to them. In today's ever-tougher competition situation it is not enough to offer reasonably good core produces. Organizations must also be able to offer good and varied service in the forms of service mentioned above. Service management is a management principal that is based on the idea that service is in the center of a business, and substantial effort is put into the development of total service offering.

Unlike a product, a service is made up of processes that are consumed at the same time as they are produced. This implies certain difficulties for quality control and marketing. Since there are no pre-fabricated products to control for quality, this process is complicated and difficult. For the customers, it is difficult to judge the value of a certain service, and it is impossible to see, test, or experience it before it has been consumed. For example, it is not until we have stayed in a hotel, got the house painted, received the consultant report, or had our hair cut that we can assess the service and its quality. The well-known sociologist Erving Goffman (1959) notes that those who run service businesses are challenged to show what they actually do for the customer. The intangible character of service makes it hard to evaluate. From an organizational perspective, it is important to somehow materialize and show what the service consists of. Many of the fixed costs that are related to a service—for example, office rent, marketing, reception, sale and developmental work—are difficult to charge. This is also true for invisible services. It is therefore fundamentally important to dramatize what the customer is offered so that all costs can be covered. For example, a hairdresser needs the customer to be confident that the haircut is executed by a master. A simple male haircut does not in reality take more than ten minutes to complete, but how many customers would pay full price for this? The hairdresser must consequently "play theater" and cut, comb, spray, compare, and trim to extend the time and in some cases also offer the customer expensive lifestyle magazines, coffee, or even wine. This dramatization helps the customer experience the service as high quality and good value, and in the best of cases, a happy customer will return for another cut. And the hairdresser can cover the costs of rent, cleaning, and supplementary training.

The perception of an organization, its image or reputation, is to a large extent based on non-material values such as civic responsibility, ethical manufacturing processes, and high quality that can be related to one organization (Levitt, 1981) and that are communicated in different situations and through different media. Some researchers believe that the third stage in organizational development is when integrated values can be offered (DeBono, 1992). The first stage is the product-oriented stage; in the second stage, competition is at the center. Values that are important in the third stage are identity and relation. In other words, the feelings that can be mediated are more important than the actual product and its qualities. These intangible values, or meta products, become more and more important. Basically, all these values are produced by and through communication.

Integrated communication

There is a rather large understanding that the division in internal and external communication is artificial, something that only exists in textbooks (Cheney, Christensen, & Dailey, 2014; Falkheimer & Heide, 2014). The concept of integrated communication was popularized at the end of 1980s, but the idea of a holistic approach to organizations' communication has existed for at least three decades. In a Swedish book entitled *The Possibilities of Information* (Sw. *Informationens möjligheter*) (Jöever, 1985), the author underlines that it is vital to take a holistic approach to information, which at this time was perceived as a central resource and an important competitive weapon. Further, it was emphasized that the information officers (which today are named communication professionals, indicative of a paradigm shift in which communication is seen as more important than information) should focus on cooperation and avoid putting up barriers to other professionals such as marketers and HR professionals.

"External communication" is regularly described as communication to target groups outside an organization—for example, customers, competitors, stakeholders, politicians, journalists, and neighbors. Thus, external communication is marketing communication in the form of advertising, crisis communication, lobbying (to try to influence political decisions) and media relations. "Internal communication" is most often described as the communication between managers and employees or between employees.

Many communication professionals have started to realize that external-directed communication—for example, TV commercials that are primarily directed at potential customers—is especially noted by their own coworkers. With commercial and external communication, such as the information on the website, some of the organizational identity is manifested and expressed. In the best of cases the coworkers' identification with the organization will be reinforced and improved and engagement with and pride in the work and organization will increase (Heide & Simonsson, 2018/in press). Analogously, internal communication flows over the organizational borders and reaches external stakeholders. Journalists may read the house magazine and find issues they wish to report to an external audience. Since the borders increasingly join together, it becomes all the more important to send out consistent messages. The idea behind integrated communication is that organizations should not send out conflicting internal and external messages. However, it is axiomatic that messages must be adapted to receivers, situations, those with relations to the organization, media, and so forth.

A need of more knowledge in communication

Despite increasing awareness of the importance of communication for organizations, many educational programs in business administration and human resources and numerous leadership courses do not contain any solid communication teaching. Already in the mid-1980s, Stephen Axley (1984) was pointing out that communication teaching in American business administration courses was based on a simplified and obsolete view of communication—in other words, the above-mentioned transmission view. This view also occurs in other educational establishments, such as medical and military schools and seminaries. This suggests that the transmission view is reproduced again and again and used in working life, and an important reason for there still being such a strong belief in information per se and so much effort put into the distribution of information.

Even though more than three decades have passed since the publication of Axley's article, there seems not to have been much change in communication teaching within business administration education. In an article published slightly more than two decades later, three communication researchers maintained that there was more or less no communication teaching in British business and management education (Cohen, Musson, & Tietze, 2005). This is quite remarkable since most subjects within the social sciences have taken both an interpretive and linguistic turn. It is especially remarkable that these turns are particularly evident within organizational studies, where there is a special interest in discourse (Alvesson & Karreman, 2013; Alvesson & Kärreman, 2000a, 2000b, 2011a). Unfortunately, there is nothing that indicates that the circumstances are different in other countries, since international, often US-based, textbooks are often used. But strategic communication is also used within education beyond pure communication education. This is naturally a development that we applaud and believe will be even stronger in the future.

The problematic internal communication

Even if more and more communication researchers have rejected the idea that it is possible to differentiate between internal and external communication, the idea still seems to be rather common in practice. All too often there are discussions of communication in terms of internal and external communication activities. The internal communication generally has lower status than external communication, which is regarded as "sexier." Among other things it can be explained by the fact that it is easier prove effects and show the return on investments of an external communication activity. The effect of a marketing effort is often limited to a fixed period, and when the organization disseminates information to certain receivers (for example all households in a city) and a certain target group (for example, fashion-conscious men). The effect of such a campaign, e.g. increased sale, is fairly easy to calculate. But the eager to assess the effects can restrict external communication to a more short-run perspective compared to internal communication. As mentioned above, modern marketing emphasizes the importance of relationship building and branding. This displacement of focus makes external communication more indirect and long-term, and the border to internal communication is no longer sharp. To produce good relations with the surrounding environment demands coworkers that identify with the core organizational values and which communicate these further to different stakeholders (Heide & Simonsson, 2011; Zerfass & Franke, 2013).

Even though the status of internal communication in organizations is not as high as external communication, there is substantial interest in internal communication among communication professionals. The theme of the annual public relations research conference Bledcom in 2011 was internal communication. An obvious impression from the conference is that more research and literature on internal communication is needed. This was confirmed by the latest survey among European communication professionals— European Communication Monitor—which shows internal communication perceived as one of the most important fields for communication professionals (Zerfass, 2017). This result has also been confirmed by other international surveys.

The eternal hunt for status

Communication professional have for a long time proposed they should have a seat on the board in corporations and public organizations. The idea is that the communication manager then can be upgraded to communication director and thereby have a greater impact on the organizational agenda and ensure that a communication perspective is ubiquitous and that the organization works with communication strategically. However, this is not always easy to realize. One problem is that the focus of many organizations is on what each coworker delivers, i.e. can concretely show what they contribute to the development of the organization and the overall result. Marketing professionals can refer to performance measurements of the latest marketing activity. This is not so easy for communication professionals. The effects of communication are almost always indirect, which makes them difficult to measure. Communication professionals often face internal legitimacy problems. They are forced to devote much time and energy to convincing the management team of the importance of communication.

Many communication managers have a problem establishing their role in the management team when there is not sufficient understanding of the communicative perspective on organizational decisions. Besides the difficulty of proving the effects of communication activities, the dominant belief is that communication and public relations involve pure craftsmanship or tactical skills rather than strategic activity.

Fortunately for communication professionals there are investigations that indicate a brighter future. The Swedish Association of Communication Professionals regularly conduct surveys among their members and the results frequently show an increasing number of more communication managers and directors with a seat at the table. These investigations indicate a steady development since year 2000. Today, approximately 70–80 percent of Swedish communication managers have earned membership in a management team. Further, the results indicate that it is more common with communication managers in management groups in public organizations. An open question is whether communication professionals can begin to drop the issue of becoming a member of the management team and instead devote time to strategic communication work that adds organizational value.

The communication professionals' efforts to raise their status are by no means unique to this group. Rather, it is a contemporary trend within almost all semi-professions—everybody wants to raise their status and become better recognized, preferably with a special professional certificate equivalent to that of physicists, psychologists, and lawyers. Advocates of professions that yearn for greater status stress in different situations and in the media that their profession contributes to society and organizations (see Ulrich, Younger, Brockbank, & Ulrich, 2013). They maintain that their profession warrants greater appreciation, higher salaries, and more attention and status. When it comes to the status of a profession, it always boils down to a comparison with other professions. In this case, it is communication professionals compared to human relations or marketing professionals. A profession's wish to control certain tasks or responsibility fields, as a way to increase the status, can be understood as a *closing strategy* (Alvesson, 2013). This involves the strong wish of a profession to have the exclusive right to certain tasks, with other professions locked out. For example, among human relations professionals there is a view that the profession should work with internal communication (Ulrich & Brockbank, 2005). However, this also involves limiting the opportunity the profession has to expand its tasks and responsibilities. Professions with a narrow and specialized direction, that monopolize a certain field, have difficulty going beyond the borders. A person that gets trained in a well-defined profession, such as a doctor, finds it harder to shift career path than, for example, a bachelor in social sciences. This means that a doctor who gets tired of being a physician and would like to change to another domain has a long way to go via new educational programs to reach the goal of a different job. Consequently, it demands great commitment and investment for the doctor to find equivalent work outside the field of medicine. This closing and locking effect is a downside of the struggle for professionalization (Alvesson, 2013). Alvesson underlines that within an organization there are many specialist units that wish to become members of a management group, work strategically, and become the CEO's favorite. As examples, Alvesson mentions production, purchasing, product development, sales, finance, information and logistics. The competition between the different specializations is, according to Alvesson, a zero-sum game. When someone wins, someone else loses. Everybody give prominence to their own work group and the unique knowledge it contributes to the organization. However, seats at the table are limited.

From the discussion above, one might question whether it is in the long run an advantageous strategy for communication professionals to get involved in a zero-sum game with marketing professionals. Maybe the fight is already lost—marketing professionals in general tend to have a stronger position in most organizations. Further, it is important to consider the possible consequences of losing to marketing professionals. Some public relations researchers are of the opinion that there is a serious risk of *marketing imperialism*—that is, when the marketing department takes care of all communication responsibilities and tasks (Cropp & Pincus, 2001; Hutton, 2001). It might therefore be wise to adopt the old English axiom: "If you can't beat them, join them." Instead of getting involved in an open conflict with marketing professionals, a smarter strategy might be to take a cooperative line and try to develop the organization's understanding of the importance of communication as a valuable organizational activity for the long term. We will like to add that this reasoning also goes for cooperation with HR. The communication, HR and marketing departments are weaker compared to the finance department, and if the "soft power" disciplines cooperate they could form a potentially strong and more influential organizational unit with greater room for action.

The importance of strategic communication

In the introduction of this book we emphasized the importance of reflexivity, i.e. of practitioners and researchers not taking things for granted or regarding them as carved in stone. As researchers in strategic communication, we would especially like to point out the crucial role that communication has as a facilitator enabling people to act and live. Without communication, we would not have a modern, organized society. Beyond functioning as a means to share messages between people, produce a feeling of being allies and muster human forces towards a common goal, communication makes it possible to produce a common social reality. We act upon the understanding we have of a situation. In other words, societies and organizations cannot exist without communication. Through communication, organizational members produce understandings of the organization, but communication is also used to project certain pictures to external stakeholders with the hope of gaining higher legitimacy in society. Through direct communication activities organizations hope, for example, to build good relations with politicians, customers and potential customers, owners, financial institutions, activist groups, and former employees. Communication is also used to improve sales or disseminate information about the brand and what it involves. The communications of an organization are in many aspects and forms strategic. In the next chapter we will discuss the concept of communication and point out some relevant communication theories. And in the following chapter we will review and discuss the concept of strategy and show that the traditional understanding of strategy is often too static and one-dimensional. Many more organizational members are strategic and work strategically than is generally thought. As Schön (1983) reminds us, to act professionally one must always reconsider old truths and think reflectively.

Part I
Fundamentals

1 What is communication?

Communication is often taken for granted as something natural and consequently not needing to be reflected upon. One may compare the relationship between human beings and communication to that between fish and water: the fish is not *conscious* of the water—the medium that creates its environment and supports its existence (Carey, 2009). Communication is as essential for human life as water is for the fish—and this is equally valid for organizations. There are researchers who claim that communication constitutes (is the primary foundation of) organizations (Cooren, Kuhn, & Cornelissen, 2011). Communication as a scientific concept is hard to discuss since it is studied and analyzed in so many ways in all kinds of discipline. Communication is a fundamental prerequisite in fields as completely different as the humanities, social science, science, engineering, and medicine. In this chapter we describe communication from a strategic communication perspective, which means that we mainly base it on material from the social sciences and sometimes the humanities.

Strategic communication may be interpreted as a direction that has its origin in three fields of knowledge: mass communication theory, organizational theory, and the humanities (language and rhetoric). From a broad perspective, strategic communication has its main base in what was previously called the sociology of communication, with a particular focus on how meaning is shared, transferred, or created between individuals, organizations, and society. During several decades from the early 1900s this field of knowledge was named mass communication research, executed by researchers in disciplines such as political science, sociology, and economic psychology. The main focus in mass communication studies was the role and effect of mass media in society (McQuail, 2010). The second field of knowledge with a clear relevance for the emergence of strategic communication is organizational theory, which was developed in fields such as sociology, psychology and, later, business administration. Organizational theory has obvious importance for organizational communication and issues concerning communicative leadership, coworkership, management, and so forth. Finally, there is a link to the humanities, especially with regard to rhetoric, linguistics, and language studies. Aristotle's art of persuasion, taught and documented around 300 BC, may be interpreted as the first text about strategic communication, even though its starting point was not organizations but the individual orator.

In this chapter we begin by describing the two fundamental perspectives of communication: *transmission* and *ritual*. Through this simplified division we can gain a better understanding of why and how communication works or does not work in different situations (Carey, 2009). The theory can be used as a thinking tool that helps us reflect upon the communication as such. Then we go through the communication theories that we believe are of particular importance for strategic communications. The theories are based on different assumptions about communication, persuasion, negotiation and dialogue.

The theory in public relations that has received the most attention has a strong relationship to the division. James Grunig and his colleagues in the United States describe it as a choice between an asymmetrical and a symmetrical approach (Grunig & Hunt, 1984), viewing public relations from a relationship angle rather than a communicative one. In this chapter we look more at this division as it has been presented and discussed by them. There are also several parallels between this division and the theory of strategic and communicative action developed by the German social philosopher Jürgen Habermas (1984). Perspective and intent are different, but both the Grunig and the Habermas models are based on the idea that mutual dialogue, reasoning to reach informed consensus, creates the ideal communication situation. Both theories are normative—that is, they provide an ideal. There are, nevertheless, considerable differences between Grunig and Habermas. First, Grunig's theory is organizational-centric and managerial, while that of Habermas is societal, democratic, and fundamentally ethical. Second, Grunig does not conceptualize a broad public sphere in his theory but defines the surrounding world as publics (or stakeholders, activist groups, and target audiences). The approach is based on a modernistic market and segmentation logic. Habermas is societal-centric, putting rational citizens and the civic community at the center. There are reasons to consider both approaches in strategic communications.

The transmission perspective

James Carey (2009) links the development of the mediated communication to the historical development of the United States, but his analyzes can be translated to other nations or contexts. When the United States began to take shape, it developed new communication modes—by writing and reading. The traditional oral communication forms, such as speeches and stories, were dependent on certain habits and abilities. Oral communication is obviously limited in scope since messages cannot move in time and space. The art of writing, and later the invention of printing in the fourteenth century (or even earlier in China), increased the ability to move messages through time and space. The oral communication tradition originated in ancient Greece. In this culture, it was viewed as important for each citizen to be able to defend themselves in courts and public assemblies, where decisions on the common good were made. In a modern nation, it is obviously impossible to maintain the ancient direct democratic ideals at a national level or even in a smaller municipality. Instead, new communication forms have been developed, step by step decompressing time and space. One way to solve the problem is to take advantage of various means of transport. Communication thus came to mean both the transport of people and goods and the transmission of information. With the help of new means of transport, such as horses and carriages and later the railroad, the emerging United States was kept together and a cultural entity could begin to develop.

In the Western world, and probably in most parts of the modernized world, the idea of communication as transmission between a sender and a recipient became a common mindset. According to Carey (2009), this has been the dominant approach since the 1920s. A transmission perspective on communication means that the transport of goods and people is equated to the transmission or transport of information between people in different contexts (groups, organizations, cities, nations, and so forth). Before the telegraph, which was established in the late 1700s, the transportation of people and information was intimately bound together. This can be explained by the fact that it was impossible to move information in any way other than distributing it by a person traveling between locations. The main focus of this perspective to communication is the movement in a geospatial room where signals and messages were spread in order to achieve control. This perspective on communication is associated with verbs like distributing, sending, forwarding and giving information to others.

The introduction of the telegraph ended the close link between transport and communication but did not take away the transport metaphor. Carey says that our idea of communication is deeply rooted in our cultural thinking and communication is often seen as the process by which messages are transmitted and distributed to different receivers. Information is equated to communication according to this line of thought. The communication process is viewed as a technical process by which a transmitter sends a message via a channel to a receiver. The process is viewed as successful when the recipient has received the message, even if the content has changed during transmission. The transmission perspective of communication can also be equated to traditional leadership (Reddy, 1993), with human intellect seen as a container for ideas and thoughts. On the basis of this approach, communication is an idea transferred from one person's brain to one another through the conduit of language. The transmitter encodes a message in linguistic form and transmits it through a medium to the receiver, which is assumed to decode the message and place it in the right place in the brain (seen as a knowledge bank) (Säljö, 1999).

The words adopted in the transmission view of communication contain particular values, so when the recipient has received the information via any medium it is assumed that she understands the message. If an organization's management detects a problem, the quick fix according to this thinking is to produce a channel and send a generic message to coworkers or external stakeholders. Based on this view, communication is something quite simple that mainly involves technology. The main challenge is to find the right words, order these as accurately as possible, and choose an effective technical medium (see Shotter, 1993). Accordingly, organizations can readily solve major communication problems (Axley, 1984). If employees appear not to have understood, it is customary to respond using one of two principles. One—*the principle of concretization*—involves sending out more information, somewhat modified and precise. Second—*the principle of repetition*—means that the transmitter resends the same information to the receiver.

In an organizational context, and for that matter in society in general, the transmission perspective is very common. We are confronted daily by massive campaigns which bombard us with different messages. If we do not understand the message first time round, according to transmission logic we will understand it if the campaign message is repeated or transmitted via other media (Twitter, Facebook, direct mail, billboards, bus advertising, newspaper, radio, television, and so forth). In organizations, different messages are sent out again and again from management to organization members (often in a top-down vertical communication process). This may involve new strategies, goals, core values, practices, or information about new challenges. The messages are disseminated through the various media available—large meetings, departmental meetings, bulletin boards, blogs, closed-circuit television (CCTV), staff magazines, internal memos, email, and intranet. The traditional focus is the formulation of an adequate and concise message and the medium choice. But despite the massive communication efforts by most organizations, it is doubtful how effective communication of this type is, and it is an open question whether messages have been understood, accepted, and internalized by the recipient, which is the aim and rational process according to linear transmission thinking.

Macnamara (2015) has conducted a major study of organizational listening involving 36 case studies in major corporate, governmental, and non-profit organizations in the UK, USA, and Australia. The results show that the transmission perspective still dominates in practice, despite the emergence of social media:

> However, research shows that organization public communication is overwhelmingly comprised of organizational speaking to disseminate organizations' messages using a transmission or broadcast model. Analysis shows that, on average, around 80 per cent of organizational resources devoted to public communication are focused on speaking (i.e. distributing the organization's information and messages). Even social media, which were developed specifically for two-way interaction, are used by organizations primarily to disseminate their messages.
>
> (Macnamara, 2015)

The ritual perspective

A completely different approach to communication is the ritual perspective. Carey (2009) suggests that a typical example of ritual communication is a sacred ceremony that unites people and creates a community. The meaning of communication according to the ritual perspective is not to exert control or persuade but rather to hold together a community over time. This community might be a group, a culture, a department, an organization, or a society. Thus, the ritual perspective of communication is closely linked to the original definition of communication, which derives from the Latin *communicare*—"to make common".

The ritual communication perspective, with strong religious connotations, is from now on termed the sensemaking perspective, since this indicates better what it really means. We humans are constantly trying to understand or make sense of our environment, our present and past. Humans strive to make sense since we need our lives (and choices or decisions) to be experienced as meaningful: "it must make sense". Basically, the human being is a communicative creature (Fisher, 1987); social interaction is a core fundament for human existence. We integrate impressions of others and are happy to share our experiences, thoughts, and ideas. Communication is fundamental to a large part of the processes through which we ascribe meaning to things and events. Previous experiences and the meaning that we ascribe to these frame our interpretation. When you find yourself in a new situation you try to understand using your interpretation frames (previous experience and knowledge). The philosopher Hans-Georg Gadamer (1989), primarily interested in the interpretation of literary art, used the concepts *understanding horizon* and *interpretation horizon* in his writing in a way that is consistent with the sensemaking perspective in communication theory. Gadamer meant that it was impossible to reach an objective interpretation of literature without taking into account the two interpretative horizons that in turn depend on tradition and history. By challenging one's own understanding and joining a dialogue around the interpretative frames, a new understanding is created. The same thing occurs during communication between two or more humans. When a new perceived situation does not fit our established interpretative frames we may either reject new possibilities of meaning or, together with others, try to find a new meaning. Our frames become more and more comprehensive. These frames make social, organizational life, as well as other people's lives, become understandable and meaningful. When you ask someone about what happened, for example, on a trip, the person will tell a coherent story that consists of various stand-alone episodes. Thus, meaning is created when we communicate. When we communicate about something, meaning (including opinion, interpretations, etc.) is constructed in interaction with both ourselves and others.

This interpretative perspective of reality is diametrically different to the perception that exists within the transmission view of communication. From a meaning perspective, there is no fixed, complete, and objective reality "out there" that can be mirrored and exactly described by language. Instead, it is assumed that it is language that helps us categorize, describe, and understand reality. With the help of language, we put different "labels" on or frames around reality, trying to understand what has happened to us. This language does not emerge spontaneously but is created and developed over time. Thus, language is a social product that we learn from childhood during our very first socialization process. According to this reasoning, language is also power and may be used to persuade others. With our different cultural backgrounds, interests, training, and experience, we tend to focus on different things and will therefore see and understand differently. As an example, one may ask how a botanist, a landscape architect, and a real estate agent each experience a garden and listen to the different linguistic categories they use (Gergen, 1999). For the same reason, citizens look at different things when a crisis in society occurs—and corporate employees see different things during an orga-nizational crisis, depending in part on their memories, interests, position, education, and experience. There is no correct way to interpret such an event; there is always another way of perceiving things.

People do not interpret themselves in a social vacuum. A great deal of the meaning-making process is done when we interpret something with other people. In an organization, employees discuss the upcoming organizational change with other employees, managers, friends, and family members and meaning emerges. In different subcultures, dominant interpretations arise over time—one can talk about interpretative frameworks—that affect our own interpretation and understanding.

The meaning of communication is determined in an interaction between two (or more) participants and not only by the transmitter (even if the trans-mitter may have more power to frame issues and events). In an ideal situation, communication is a form of dialogue, a joint effort in which equal parties strive to achieve mutual understanding. In reality, communication processes in organizations (and societies) are effected by power in different ways: some actors have more information, stronger positions due to different factors, and more strategic communicative resources.

Both perspectives matter

Both transmission and sensemaking perspectives have their merits in different situations and contexts, even if the sensemaking perspective is based on a human communication approach that is more relevant if one want to create under-standing and common knowledge or meaning. But it is important to emphasize that we need both approaches. One of them does not necessarily exclude the other, since they focus on different aspects of the communication process. The transmission perspective is still needed in some situations. One example is during a crisis situation, where it is important that instructive information is transmitted to all involved actors at once. In this situation one must obviously construct the message in a way that is understandable to all relevant people, but there is no time to develop any form of dialogue or feedback system. Another example of when a transmission perspective is optimal is when an organization communicates simple, instructive, descriptive information to some of their internal and external stakeholders. This form of information may relate to issues such as the date of a meeting, budget outcomes, etc.; basically, information with very limited or no interpretative aspects. This information may also be transmitted via so-called poor media (e.g. by email) with weak possibilities for feedback, discussion, and so forth. Still, one must be aware that historically the problem has been that the transmission perspective has completely dominated how, in many organizations, all forms of communication are planned and executed, particularly with regard to strategic communication efforts.

The transmission and sensemaking perspectives may also be connected to different communication strategies at a higher level. Either an actor intends to use information to influence and instruct a group of people in the direction decided by the organization's management, or the actor uses sensemaking strategies to influence and instruct the management of the organization in the direction that mirrors different stakeholder interests. The first intention follows what may be called a *persuasion model,* since it is entirely based on organizational goals beyond the reach of stakeholders. This does not mean that the model is applied without feedback. But the environment is considered from a more limited perspective in the sense that only the direct and obvious relationships are taken into account. This means that a corporation only considers feedback from one pre-defined and constructed stakeholder group, such as customers or retailers. For a public organization, this strategy may instead involve feedback from a pre-defined citizen group. This organization-centric strategic communication approach implicitly means that stakeholders are talked to, not talked with. The role and task of communication professionals following the persuasion model is to be an implementer, or a producer and distributor of messages based on decisions that have already been taken. The second, contrasting, intention follows what may be called an *adaptation model.* This model implies a listening organization in which objectives and decisions are formulated together with different stakeholders in relation to their values, attitudes, behaviors, and trends. The communication professional here is a strategic key player whose job is to listen to and represent the stakeholder environment.

The adaption model is idealistic and in practice the line of persuasion is not as clear as it is in theory. It is not possible for an organization to fully adapt to all employees, customers, citizens' groups, interest organizations, activist groups, etc. In reality, the practice of strategic communication is more of a negotiation between different interests, audiences, and goals.

It is possible to connect this discussion with a role model for strategic public relations practitioners that has been developed by Gregory and Willis (2013). The four-by-four model consists of four organizational levels common to all organizations (functional, corporate, stakeholder/value chain, and societal) and four strategic public relations strands (brand, leadership, core competence, and planning) undertaken at all levels. The stakeholders and stakeholder networks are viewed as fundamental: "The stakeholders ultimately determine and define the nature of an organization, providing its license to operate and without whose cooperation it will cease to exist" (Gregory & Willis, 2013, p. 35).

At the societal level the role of the communication practitioner is to contribute contextual intelligence that "helps the organizations' leaders to make sense of an external environment that is in a permanent state of flux" (Gregory & Willis, 2013, p. 36). This role is called "orienter" and may be connected to the sensemaking perspective. At the corporate level the role of the public relations practitioner is to "build reputational and relational capital needed for an organization to meet its objectives ... ." This includes coaching organizational managers and providing them with intelligence about stakeholders before decisions are made and communicating with stakeholders (Gregory & Willis, 2013, p. 37). This role is named "navigator" and may also be connected to a sensemaking perspective, but from an organization-centric point of view. At the value-chain level the primary stakeholders (e.g. customers or employees) are put at the center. "The role of the public relations function is being attuned to and representing all these 'close' stakeholder perspectives, internal and external, to senior managers in the organization is critical to organizational success" (Gregory & Willis, 2013, p. 39). This role is termed "catalyst" and may be seen as a combination of the transmission and sensemaking perspectives. Finally, at the functional level the role of the public relations practitioner is to plan and align communication activities with organizational mission, vision, and general strategy. This means that being an "implementer" is closely linked to a transmission perspective on communications.

Theories of communication

Giving an overview of different communication theories is a gigantic task, for the simple reason that there are lots of theories. In this section we have chosen some theories that we find of core relevance for strategic communications. From a general approach, communication may be described, analysed, and understood at four different levels. First, at the *individual* level, which contain ideas, models, and theories that have their primary base in psychology. Second, at the *group* level, which has its primary base in social psychology (how the social context effect individual characteristics) or linguistics. Third, at the *organizational* level, which focuses on social communication processes in what is sometimes defined as goal-oriented collectives of people with predefined (often professional) roles. This level may involve use of sociological, linguistic, and social-psychological research. Finally, at a *society* level (e.g. cities or national states), which primarily involves the use of sociology, anthropology, political science, and media studies. Every level of communication may be described and analyzed from different perspectives. In any case, it is clear that we must always make a selection on the basis of interest and understand that there are always other perspectives that may produce relevant insights. From a strategic communication point of view, the organizational and society levels may be viewed as of core interest. But the boundary between the individual and group levels is not always easy to draw.

Rosengren (2000) made a similar division between intrapersonal, interpersonal, group, organizational, and societal levels. The intrapersonal level (communication with oneself) may be problematic since this form of communication does not involve any other human. Rosengren believes that the intrapersonal level becomes pointless if it also includes psychological processess such as perception and cognition. But it is hard to dismiss the intrapersonal level when it comes to more explicit forms of interpersonal communication in social media. Time and space are also crucial elements of all forms of communication.

The first communication theory: rhetoric

Aristotle's (1959) (384–322 BC) text *Ars Rhetorica* may be considered the first scientifically formulated communication theory, with a focus on the art of convincing or persuading. The ancient rhetorical experts, who have a lot of similarities with contemporary communication consultants, were named sophists (of Greek *sophia*, "wisdom"). The sophists sold their services as advisors and taught their customers how to argue their case effectively. The philosopher Plato opposed the sophists' relativistic views of truth, calling rhetoric a doctrine of manipulation with the sole purpose of winning argumentation, not telling the truth.

Rhetoric was a separate academic subject in parts of the world for many centuries, but it was challenged during both the Enlightenment of the 1700s and the Romantic movement of the 1800s. During the postwar period in the 1900s there was a renaissance of rhetoric in the academic world. The same renaissance is evident in society in general; for example, rhetorical experts are now often asked by journalists to analyze political speeches or crisis communication tactics. But to this day, rhetoric is still often used as a negative term adjacent to "spin", propaganda, or manipulation—suggesting unethical communication with little or no relationship to truth. Ancient rhetoric is divided into three different genres of speech: deliberative (political), forensic (judicial), and epidectic (ceremonial). Within strategic communication, especially public relations and crisis communication, there are strong links to theories of how to defend reputation during and after a crisis—one example is the image repair strategy (Benoit, 1995).

Aristotle systematized rhetorical concepts, genres, and rhetoric planning phases (invention, arrangement, style, memory, and delivery) and highlights three main elements present to varying degrees in different rhetorical-communicative situations. First, *ethos*, which is related to the speaker's credibility. Credibility is not only created in a speech situation, but Aristotle mentioned three factors that may support ethos: *fronesis* (the orator is perceived as intelligent), *arete* (the orator is perceived as a person of high moral judgement), and *eunoia* (the orator is perceived as a person who wants the best for his/her fellows). Second, *pathos,* dealing with emotions that the speaker is trying to create and the audience to experience. This may involve the orator showing his or her own feelings, using emotional symbols, anecdotes, or examples. Third, *logos,* which concerns the rational arguments and logical reasoning that is used by an orator. Put simply this involves the use of facts, figures, linear logical reasoning, and perhaps references to scientific sources. By using eloquent language (Lat. *elocutio*) and various rhetorical figures such as metaphors, analogies, or parallelisms, the orator tries to influence his audience by combining these different means. The systematics that Aristotle created still have relevance and can be compared with modern models and formulas for strategic communication, marketing, and so forth. The orator may just as well be an organization and in modern times a new field of organizational rhetoric has evolved.

Rhetoric is both a theory of human persuasive communication and an arsenal of tools for people who want to understand the resources that are available in a rhetorical-communicative situation. The linguistic focus that is the basis of rhetoric has had a scientific revival, sometime named the "linguistic turn", with clear links to poststructuralist and postmodern theories (e.g. discourse analysis) that the social sciences developed during the late 1900s.

Transmission and mass communication theories

Very few contemporary communication scholars now refer to the communication models developed during the 1940s and 1950s. During this period there was a scientific-technical knowledge ideal aiming to create a single universal model that could explain all forms of communication. But the two theories that are usually attributed to this belief in universal systems for the technological transfer of information have been subjected at times to naïve and ahistoric criticism. This was true for the "The Mathematical Theory of Communication", published in *The Bell System Technical Journal* by the researchers Shannon and Weaver (1949). This theory deals with mathematical conditions for signal transmission via electronic media on the basis of a division between transmitter, encoding, signal, noise, receiver, and feedback. Shannon and Weaver coined several key concepts incorporated into social and behavioral communication research. The criticism that later generations of communication researchers raised against the model is misdirected: the purpose of the model was not to describe interpersonal communication (Jansson, 2009). In contrast, this research has been of great importance for the development of digital communication decades later.

The theory developed by the political scientist and communication scholar Harold D. Lasswell also met with this sort of response. From the 1920s Lasswell conducted groundbreaking studies on mass media and propaganda. Lasswell (1948) described a now classic formula of five elements that could be analyzed: *Who says what to whom by which channel and with what effect?* This formula has since been criticized for being based on the same simplistic approach to communication as Shannon and Weaver's model, but the fact is that Lasswell was mainly interested in the study of propaganda and his studies had a solid reality-based background. The role of mass media and propaganda during the first and second world wars can hardly be underestimated, even if the belief that media had a one-directional powerful effect was later problematized (McQuail, 2010). And the simplified formula does not completely illustrate Lasswell ideas. He also highlighted that the division was problematic and that he viewed communication as an integrated process. During the 1900s there were increased concerns in society regarding mass communication effects. During this era, mass communication content was created by professional sources, advertising agencies, newspapers, political campaigners, and so forth. Mass media were viewed as technical channels for distribution and the receivers (defined as public opinion or an audience and later also as target groups) were for a long time seen as passive and homogenous. But media and mass communication scholars gradually realized that the effects of mass communication were not at all conclusive. One of the milestones in mass communication research was set by the sociologist Lazarsfeld and his research team, based on the results of their major studies of media influence on political elections and voters during the 1940s and 1950s (Katz & Lazarsfeld, 1955; Lazarsfeld, Gaudet, & Berelson, 1968). Lazarsfeld's research problematized the established idea that media had a direct and unidirectional effect on political attitudes and behaviors. Instead, the empirical studies demonstrated three types of media effect on election campaigns, which could well be compared with communication forms other than the political forms of communication campaigns or actions (Strömbäck & Kiousis, 2011): activation (of underlying values and attitudes), enforcement (which accounted for most voters), and inversion (which was a relatively modest effect). Lazarsfeld's studies also led to the creation of the two-step flow of communication model, which, simply put, means that interpersonal communication, or discussions between people, have a much stronger effect on attitudes and behaviors than mass communication. The key players in these processes are so-called *opinion leaders*, defined as people who have higher media use, are considered trustworthy because they are similar to others, and are more savvy and social than others in the field. The two-step flow of communication has been considerably criticized, partly because it was established before the breakthrough of television and other new media (such as social media), which has made the process more multifaceted and complex, and partly due to the fact that the division between passive followers and active opinion leaders is not reliable, with value changes in later generations leading to reduced confidence in authorities and opinion leaders. Despite this, opinion leaders are undeniably important in all forms of strategic communication and are a classic tactic of influence.

There is a direct link between the two-step flow of communication model from the 1940s and the increased interest in business and research for so-called *influencers* in social media. Uzunoğlu and Misci Kip (2014) conclude that social media converts the two-step flow model into a multistep flow theory where each receiver is also a potential transmitter. Influencers are hard to define and do not fit with early definitions of opinion leaders. Basically, influencers are connected to large networks of people (with common lifestyles, interests, and values) through social media such as blogs, Twitter, or Instagram. They may be young or old, professionals or non-professionals, already established celebrities or not. In any case, influencers need to be considered authentic and personal. In the field of public relations, the impact of personal influencers is nothing new even if social media have changed the roles and processes. In marketing, where promotional advertising has traditionally been a core platform, the role of influencers has led to the establishment of sub-disciplines such as influencer marketing. Marketers map important influencers who have developed strong personal brands as well as huge networks and try to assign them as channels for promoting products and services. The influencers may get rich but risk losing credibility when they make these agreements, especially if their integrity is damaged.

The agenda-setting theory is another classical mass communication theory, based on empirical studies of how people are influenced by political opinion formation in the media (McCombs & Shaw, 1972). The agenda-setting theory shows, among other things, that there is strong correlation between what the mass media reports and what people consider to be important issues—in other words, the mass media more or less decides what is discussed in public. But the mass media does not control *how* people interpret the content of the media. There have now been hundreds of studies of agenda setting and the theory has been questioned (e.g. criticized for being too simple and causal and viewing audiences as rather passive), but the main conclusions that McComb and Shaw drew may still be considered largely valid.

Translating the agenda-setting theory into an organizational context, many leaders and executives probably recognize the reasoning. It is rather easy to influence what employees are talking about in an organization, much more difficult to make all employees think the same way or influence their interpretations—and some people emerge as strong opinion leaders in these processes. The fact that most people reinforce their pre-existing values and attitudes can in turn be explained by the theory of cognitive dissonance (Festinger, 1957). This theory is based on humans' need for psychological balance or equilibrium, which means that we rationalize our choices or decisions retrospectively. Simply put, most people prefer to support their choices or decisions, not to change them. It is human to discard or ignore information that does not confirm what you already know or think or to interpret information in such a way that you can defend your values, attitudes, or actions. Basically, this is a psychological defense mechanism, which means that we organize our image of reality in such a way that it becomes consistent with our actions so that they appear accurate and beneficial. An example might be a manager who decides to purchase a new intranet system. When launched, more and more employees complain that it does not work properly. The manager is listening, but does not want to hear the negative information. The manager is selective and only retrieves information that confirms the rightness of his decision. Not until the negative information has increased to the strength of a hurricane will the manager realize that he or she is wrong. Another example may be obtained from crisis situations, where there can be very considerable pressure on individuals. During crises, the media tend to search for scapegoats who they can claim are responsible for what went wrong. It is common that the people in leading positions avoid all liability, even if they are actually responsible. This behavior can of course be strategic, but it can also be explained by dissonance theory—that is, it is a way to rationalize what has happened in order to create consistency between thought and action. As a communication professional, it is important to understand that people reinforce the attitudes and behaviors they already prefer rather than create brand new ones. This applies equally to managers, employees, customers, and citizens.

Communication as co-creation

The established communication theories presented above have been completed and further developed in different ways. In recent decades, communication research has become more and more characterized by a participatory perspective. The division between sender and receiver (with a strong focus on channels and distribution) is challenged and replaced by a contextual, sensemaking, and interactive perspective. The technological development is, of course, central to this communication-theoretical shift. Due to digitalization, the structure of the mass communication theory is partly eroded. Mass communication theories assume that certain institutions (organizations such as newspaper or other media companies, advertising or public relations agencies, public authorities, etc.) own and control the production and distribution systems. Reaching a large group of people with a message was the essential work of professional communicators who had both knowledge of and access to these systems. This is now no longer the case. In principle, anyone who has access to a computer or mobile can now make movies, texts and so on, publish them on different social media platforms, and reach a large group of people beyond time and space. One might even say that every individual is a potential media company. There are of course those who have a highly optimistic view of this development, which means that all people are now participants and media producers, eroding old hierarchies and power relationships: "Here comes everybody" (Shirky, 2009). But there are also skeptics and critics who argue that the power of information in a society or organization has never been evenly distributed and that the new digital technology primarily allows increased monitoring, new forms of propaganda, and commercial exploitation: "Corporate social media are not a realm of user/prosumer [prosumer: producer/consumer] participation, but a realm of Internet prosumer commodification and exploitation. The exploitation of Internet prosumer labor is one of many tendencies of contemporary capitalism" (Fuchs, 2013).

In the field of marketing changes a major change has taken place over the last decades due to the new communication opportunities offered by digital media and data. Traditional marketing is based on the exchange and trans-action of physical products such as cars, furniture, and other consumer goods. As the service sector and the supply of services has grown, product-oriented marketing has become less important. Researchers like Christian Grönroos (1994) were early critics of traditional marketing models that mainly focus on an efficient production process and have a unilateral business perspective. To provide an alternative view, Grönroos launched the concept of relationship marketing, which puts the customer, not the product, at the center.

Based on these thoughts, Stephen Vargo and Robert Lusch (2004, 2015) developed a new perspective in marketing—a service-dominant logic. It focuses on consumers and long-term relationships and has a developed view of the exchange process. According to the new logic, consumers are co-creators of value. Value creation does not end when the product is handed over to the consumer but continues when the consumer uses the product. Marketing today means much more than developing, promoting, and delivering pro-ducts. Vargo and Lusch argue that there is a similar paradigm shift in both marketing and communication research and practice, as the traditional func-tionalist, mechanistic, and product-oriented model is left behind for a more humanistic and relationship-based model. In the new paradigm, the impor-tance of communication processes is emphasized, especially the need for dia-logue and for corporations to give consumers a direct answer to the questions they ask. The service-dominant logic is basically a value-based model in which all actors are perceived as important resources. C. K. Prahalad and Venkatram Ramaswamy (2003) have had a significant impact with similar ideas in the field of innovation and production development. They argue that neither value nor innovation can be created from a purely business and product-oriented starting point, especially not with increasingly tough global compe-tition. Consumers have more choice than ever before but are often less satisfied, which is of course a big challenge for corporations. According to Prahalad and Ramaswamy, the digital media is both a factor behind the paradigm shift in marketing and an important medium for creating and maintaining relation-ships with consumers and thus jointly producing value. Through the use of digital media, consumers have gained greater power. This is partly because access to information is now much more open than before and partly because different customer communities come together and can exert influence on companies. Furthermore, customers can disseminate their views about pro-ducts they are dissatisfied with or tell different stakeholders how they have been treated by business representatives, which in itself may pose a threat to companies. In other words, companies must adapt to this situation, not least because the consumers' experience of a company, its activities and products or services are of major importance for the value-adding processes, innovations, strategies, and leadership.

A first step, according to Prahalad and Ramaswamy (2004), is to realize the changing consumer role, which has gone from isolated to interconnected, from unconscious to informed, and from passive to active. The next step is to establish a value-creation system according to the DART model (see Figure 1.1). The acronym DART stands for dialogue, access, risk-benefits, and transparency. This model challenges managements' and managers' previously strong position with regard to, for example, access to information and control of the dialogue with customers.

According to the DART model, four building blocks are needed to understand and create shared values. The first is *dialogue*. Prahalad and Ramaswamy emphasize that dialogue involves more than just listening to customers. There must be a reciprocity, where both parties learn and communicate as equals with the goal of developing and improving together. A positive side effect of dialogue is that it provides good conditions for creating and maintaining a loyal community. Later research (e.g. Gustafsson, Kristensson, & Witell, 2012) confirms that communication and interaction between consumers and companies is a key aspect of achieving successful collaborative products. *Access* is the second building block in the model. Prahalad and Ramaswamy emphasize that successful companies give customers access to their "libraries", data about the production process, etc. *Risk*

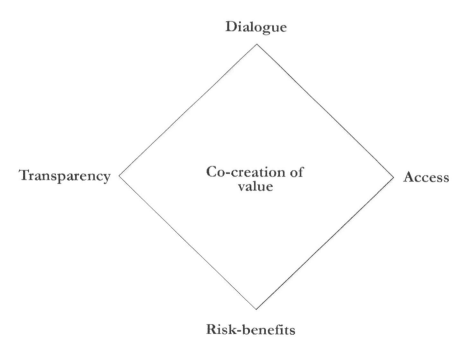

Figure 1.1 The DART model
Source: Prahalad and Ramaswamy (2004).

assessment is the third building block. One might think that consumers should also share the risk if they are co-creators. Prahalad and Ramaswamy think this is going a little too far, but they point out that it is important to communicate the risks that exist. The last building block is *transparency,* which has increased significantly in recent years, partly due to the emergence of digital media and partly because external stakeholders require greater transparency. The requirement for transparency from consumers and other stakeholders is also linked to the debates about sustainability and corporate social responsibility (CSR). Together, according to Prahalad and Ramaswamy, these building blocks create better opportunities for companies to engage consumers and, at best, communication with consumers can lead to new products and services—that is, new values may be created.

Still, research shows that only a few contemporary organizations really open up and are transparent. One can also strongly question what kind of and whose transparency we are talking about (Christensen, 2002). The information published on the company website is usually strategically selected, from a management perspective. Employee opinions, if different from those of management, are seldom if ever published on the web. Furthermore, research has shown that the digital media dialogues are utilized to only a limited extent (Santi & Kyoichi, 2012).

The models of co-creation can be seen as expressions of a sharing discourse. At the same time, the theories mentioned above clearly reflect the perspective of companies. A critical theorist like Habermas, whose work we will present soon, would probably view co-creation as a hidden strategic act. We still believe that we live in a time that could be described as experiencing a communicative paradigm shift: from the transmission model to a participatory or co-creation model (sometimes conceptualized by such similar terms as share, open, access, and dialogue). In strategic communication (but mostly in public relations), basic communication theory has received rather little attention, but the interest is increasing. The break from the transmission perspective has become clearer in the last decades. As an example, Botan and Taylor (2004) emphasize the emergence of a collective perspective in public relations:

> The co-creational perspective sees publics as co-creators of meaning and communication as what makes it possible to agree to shared meanings, interpretations and goals. This perspective is long term in its orientation and focuses on relationships among publics and organizations.
>
> (p. 652)

The characterization of publics and the transformation of the public sphere

Grunig and Hunt (1984), core contributors to research in public relations, initially analyzed what distinguished different publics that end up in conflict with organizations (the concept "public" is somewhat similar to the concept "stakeholder", which has its origin in business and management research). In this context, a public is not the same thing as a professional public, but rather about spontaneous formations of people constructed in relation to a problem or dispute that exists or is created between an organization and it's surroundings. A situational example may be when environmental organizations respond to increase in emissions from an industry. Another example may be when a healthcare administration is assigned responsibility when individual healthcare workers to mistreat patients. A third example may be when a food company is attacked in the media because their products are considered to contribute to obesity among the population. Grunig and Hunt defined four different publics based on degree of engagement and problem involvement:

- *Non-publics:* Potential groups of people who are not affected by a problem and thus have no problem involvement or engagement.
- *Latent publics*: Groups of people who can have a high problem involvement but lack engagement. In other words, typically dissatisfied but passive actors who do not consider themselves able to do anything that affects the problem.
- *Conscious publics*: Groups with both high problem involvement and potential engagement. It is not entirely certain that they will act, but the possibility exists.
- *Active publics*: Groups with high problem involvement that are directly affected by the problem and who are strongly engaged. The groups have also organized themselves and established strategies and tactics to confront the organization that is considered responsible for the problem.

The publics are not static but can be seen as different stages in a process. An organization that has no knowledge of which publics might become active and neglects latent and conscious publics runs the greatest risk of ending up in a "situation" with active publics. When the organization is challenged by an active public, for example through different opinion activities (demonstrations, debate articles, Twitter storms, etc.), there is quite a bit to do. The problem has already been defined by the external publics. Studies of reactive defense strategies in confidence crises that arise indicate that it is usually most effective to acknowledge the problem and apologize (Benoit, 1995). We will return to trust and advocacy strategies later in the book.

New media technologies, forms of social organization, and an increased focus on single issues have led to an increase in active publics, as well as the speed with which they organize themselves (Hearit, 1999). Grunig (2009) believes that the theory of publics and the public relations models (presented later) developed by him and his colleagues are still valid—and that the increased interactivity between organizations and its surroundings implies that journalism has becomes less important and that the possibilities for symmetrical communication are increasing. Despite this normative optimistic attitude, Grunig also states that practice does not change so quickly:

> The new digital media have dialogical, interactive, relational, and global properties that make them perfectly suited for a strategic management paradigm of public relations—properties that one would think would force public relations practitioners to abandon their traditional one way, message oriented, asymmetrical and ethnocentric paradigm of practice. However, history shows that when new media are introduced communicators tend to use them in the same way that they used the old media.
>
> (Grunig, 2009, p. 6)

Grunig also means that organizations now have to use public relations to participate in the discussions that are created and exist among different publics (Grunig, 2009). The management perspective that permeates this reasoning is in sharp contrast to the ideas and theories developed by probably the best-known philosopher who focused on the public sphere, Jürgen Habermas. The social philosopher Habermas is a constantly referenced source for issues concerning the public sphere. Habermas had as his background the so-called Frankfurt school, which began its critical research in the 1930s. The Frankfurt school was not really a school, rather it was a collective term for a variety of researchers, all of which applied a critically theoretical and frequently pessimistic perspective on modern capitalist society. The fundamental ideas were developed in the book *Dialectic of Enlightenment*, written by Theodor Adorno and Max Horkheimer (1944). In this highly critical text, the authors find that the values that characterized early modern society—rationality, freedom, and progress—have been replaced, due to the increased influence of capitalism in all sectors of society, by their opposites. Inspired by so-called neo-Marxism and characterized by the authors' personal experience of a totalitarian society and its ideologies, Adorno and Horkheimer criticized both Nazi and American popular culture. Habermas belongs to a later (third) generation of critical theory and has in particular developed theories of transformations of the public sphere and communicative action. Habermas (1989) *The Structural Transformation of the Public Sphere: An Inquiry into a Category of Bourgeois Society,* published in 1962 as his doctoral dissertation, is driven by a critical emancipatory ideal. Habermas's ideal is harmonic, equal, and rational communication between community citizens, with everyone participating. In his analysis he is particularly interested in the importance and functionality of mass media. Simply put, he has a pessimistic view of the role of media in societal development. In his analysis he evokes a historical epoch and cultural environment where an ideal rational public sphere free from interference existed: the bourgeois public sphere that developed in the eighteenth century in cafes and other public spaces. In this sphere newspapers, magazines, and books were read and discussed from a public interest perspective. Habermas means that after this period the mass media has been integrated into the capitalist (or totalitarian) community of conglomerates that increasingly regards the public as a group of customers instead of equal citizens. Journalism has been commercialized according to the same reasoning. Public relations as well as advertising are mentioned as examples and expressions of this unfortunate development.

Habermas's idealization of the bourgeois public sphere of the eighteenth century has been roundly criticized, not least because this forum belonged exclusively to a masculine elite. One of the other main counter arguments is that Habermas's theory is based on an excessive confidence in rationality. Bauman commented on this confidence by likening Habermas's ideals to an academic sociology seminar, where everyone participates and all arguments are tested correctly (Bauman & May, 2001), which may sound like an academic Utopia but is hardly human society.

Habermas believes that the public sphere is a mediating structure between political and private systems. In order to adapt Habermas's theory to public relations, Inger Jensen (2001) distinguishes three public processes (the last of them lacks support from Habermas's theories and is added by Jensen):

- *Literary public processes.* These processes accommodate different forms of culture and expression that occur in the public sphere. Basically, these processes consist of different types of reflection among individuals and groups of people. In literary processes we reflect on ourselves using a constructed world. In practice, there is no difference between high and low culture; these processes include all forms of art and literature and are to be found in popular movies and games as well as art galleries and novels. Through these processes, opinions, attitudes, and identities are created.
- *Political public processes.* In these processes, societal problems and solutions are identified. Criticism of or demands on regulations at local, regional, national, or transnational levels are at the center. This is partly an institutionalized process in the form of government, parliament, and other legal actors, partly a civil and unregulated process with citizens and various social and political movements. The media can be regarded as a filter between these processes.
- *Organizational public processes.* These processes are highly relevant to strategic communication. Here are processes that aim at creating legitimacy and identity for organizations in relation to other organizations and societal processes. The starting point is that organizations form part of the public sphere and act on its terms. The intentions vary, and include everything from building organizational brands, creating attention and demonstrating social responsibility to influencing regulatory processes.

Asymmetry, symmetry or both

Within public relations research, one of the core fields of strategic communication, the five different public relations models that James Grunig and his colleagues developed during the 1980s and 1990s in the so-called Excellence project have been paradigmatic for the field (see Table 1.1). The models are mainly based on quantitative surveys of three hundred organizations in the United States, Canada, the United Kingdom, and at a later stage in a number of other countries in Asia and Europe (Dozier, Grunig, & Grunig, 1995). The Excellence project researchers emphasize that the five models can be regarded as historically based, and that the latter models may be seen as offering both strategic and ethical ideals for practice. From a scientific theoretical perspective, the project is rooted in a system theory tradition which here implies that the purpose is to create balance and harmony between organizations and society through public relations. In other words, communication is about the management of these relationships in order to primarily benefit the organization's best interests. The first question concerns whether direct contacts between people are in focus (including interactive mediation, for example by telephone or e-mail) or by mass media or other media (for example, by blogs or newsletters within a larger organization). The possibilities of creating the conditions for ideal symmetrical communication increase with direct contacts, while mass media as such are considered one way-oriented as channels. It is also a fact that the latter models are mostly about situations when there is a potential dispute between an organization and its publics, while the early publicity model is based on the lack of knowledge about something.

The publicity model is considered to represent the practice of the first epoch, especially in the United States, connected to the emergence of critical journalism and lack of public confidence in large companies. In practice. public relations was often the same thing as dubious crisis management ("damage control"). Some critical scholars (e.g. Ewen, 1996) find this form of

Table 1.1 Five models for public relations

	Publicity model	*Information model*	*Asymmetric two-way model*	*Symmetric two-way model*	*Game model— Mixed motive*
Aim	Propaganda	Dissemination of information	Scientific persuasion	Mutual understanding	Negotiation win-win
Process	One-way truth not essential	One-way truth important	Two-way truth important	Two-way truth important	Two-way perspective
Model	Sender–receiver	Sender–receiver	Feedback-system	Group to group network	Sender–sender
Effect	Exposure	Distribution	Range attitudes	Qualitative understanding	Diplomatic agreement

Source: Grunig and Hunt (1984) and Dozier, Grunig, and Grunig (1995), adapted by the authors.

public relations—with little or no relationship to the truth—is still common. Under everyday conditions the primary purpose of public relations according to the publicity model is to gain media attention and coverage. This form of public relations, or PR, is what many people associate the concept with: creating spectacular stories or events that gain massive attention. Indeed, it was the "experience" industry of the past (circus, theater, etc.) that developed early public relations. The publicity model still applies in fields such as the entertainment industry and politics and during wars and conflicts. The basic problem is ethical in that the purpose is considered pre-eminent; there is no truth requirement. From an applied perspective there are three fundamental problems:

- Publicity says very little about the actual effects on attitudes and behavior.
- Maximum publicity rarely produces long-term effects, only short-term effects.
- The model is founded in a transmission perspective of communication, neglecting interpretative dimensions as well as the complexity of communication as such.

This is not say that the publicity model should be rejected: if exposure is based on truthfulness, there is the chance of some long-term benefit. Based on the persuasive model, exposure is of course important in the first part of a communication process. But publicity must be put in its context and integrated as part of an overall strategy

The information model is not as focused on media attention and journalistic exposure. However, the same persuasion model is the starting point. But the effects are measured slightly closer to the target groups, as distribution and reach. For example, if the sender has successfully transferred a brochure to the recipient's mailbox or placed a product promotion on a Facebook log, the target has been reached. According to Grunig and other researchers, the model is particularly common in public information activities. Strategic development, adaptation to group or individual levels, and evaluation are valued less highly than distribution measures. An assumption is that many organizations can recognize themselves in this model. It is difficult to get media attention so the focus moves to producing and distributing brochures, leaflets, or digital ads to unclear target groups. The information model has two fundamental problems from an applied perspective:

- The lack of strategy, target group adjustment, and evaluation leads to weak effects.
- The model is based on a one-way communication view, overvalues the importance of channels and content, and neglects sensemaking and interpretations.

The asymmetrical two-way model is a strategic model, which in practice means that the sender is more interested in feedback than in the previous models. It constitutes a blend between persuasion and adaptation. The publicity model is about pure exposure and the information model about distribution; with this third model the sender investigates where the message lands. In concrete terms, the sender conducts surveys (typically using quantitative methods) in order to find out which channels and messages work for different target groups. Measuring attitudes are crucial for this model. The model is most often used for targeted information or promotional campaigns and less rarely when it comes to media attention. Media publicity may be measured in several interesting ways, but in practice it has been common to focus on counting message distribution, not effects on attitudes. This is strange since there is a long tradition of media effects research and theories about how media content is interpreted differently depending on context, situation, and audience. However, there are also criticisms of this model since it is still very sender-oriented and does not takie into account situations where the subject or message requires other forms of communication that provide greater scope for negotiation and dialogue between two parties.

The symmetrical two-way model is based on this dialogue ideal, where transmitters and recipients as concepts are replaced by two equal parties. But one may question whether dialogue is a valid concept for strategic communication that in itself has a persuasive purpose. Dialogue is created through open-ended conversations. According to the philosopher Martin Buber, real dialogue means seeing the value of each other's experiences and regarding each other as subjects, not objects (Falkheimer & Heide, 2003). The symmetry model also received criticism for being utopian and rather obscure—neglecting issues of power that are unavoidable in practice. In any case, attempts at symmetrical communication are a necessity in situations where there is conflict. It also has validity in situations where there is some kind of crisis.

The mixed motive model, inspired by game theory, is a compromise between symmetry and asymmetry and is based on negotiation as a central concept. The starting point is similar to that in the symmetric model: there is a conflict or differing judgements. A solution can only be found when the two (of more) parties give up something and find common ground. When both parties give up something, cooperation is achieved and both win something (win-win).

The public relations models should not only be seen as a history of development. Grunig believes that all models have some applicable relevance, depending on an organization's purpose or context (Grunig, 1992). For example, initial media coverage is often a prerequisite for an effective long-term campaign (provided that the other models are applied in accordance with a well-thought-out strategy). Based on his studies, Grunig considers that the first two models are mainly used by large conservative organizations that have a dominant view of their surroundings and do not see communication as relational but as the transmission of predetermined norms and messages. Two-way models allow the environment some influence but still on the organization's terms.

Although the publicity model was more common in the early 1900s than today, there is no doubt that it still exists. Digitalization has led to new propaganda possibilities—at the same time as opportunities for two-way communication have increased. There are many contemporary examples of new forms of propaganda that may be partly linked to the publicity model. One example is the social media strategies of the terrorist group Daesh (also Islamic State or IS). Daesh developed a complex media and communication system that combines old propaganda and publicity tactics with contemporary communication strategies. By using several channels (a multi-channel strategy), a strong narrative driven by a core goal (to create a caliphate), and visual communication with intertexts to established action genres and inviting fans and co-members to take part in the productions, Daesh has created a transnational brand (Nissen, 2014; Falkheimer, 2016). By posting a massive number of messages and content in different channels the messages are spread to all stakeholders.

Strategic and communicative action

The dichotomy between transmission and sensemaking approaches is of core relevance for strategic communication theory. Concepts and ideas about asymmetrical and symmetrical communication, target groups and publics, and the public sphere are also at the center of the field. Leaving strategic communications and public relations theories aside, there are good reasons for learning more about societal communication and the public sphere. The best-known scholar in this field is the German sociologist and philosopher Jürgen Habermas. Habermas's communication theory is based on a division between strategic and communicative actions (Habermas, 1984). Strategic action is goal-oriented, persuasive, and instrumental, while communicative action is oriented towards understanding and consensus. The goal of strategic action is to quickly and efficiently achieve external goals. The objective of communicative action is rational and mutual understanding through critical discussion in order to coordinate actions. We can thus see the strategic act of Grunig's asymmetric models and the communicative behavior of the symmetrical model. The basic question is whether it is possible to practice or plan for communicative action in strategic communication. Following Habermas's theory, strategic communication in itself is obviously strategic, not communicative. Habermas would probably claim that when strategic communication professionals emphasize concepts such as symmetry and rational discourse, they are in reality pursuing a hidden strategic purpose. He means that due to the development of modern capitalism, most societies have become colonized by strategic action. Figure 1.2 illustrates Habermas's communication theory.

In accordance with strategic action, the organizational intention is to control and influence the environment. Through different functions and strategies, organizations try to anticipate future and potential behaviors. A typical strategic approach is to try to identify and classify different audiences (such as target groups, stakeholders, or activist groups), as Grunig does. The next step is purely tactical. Various methods are used to control and influence the

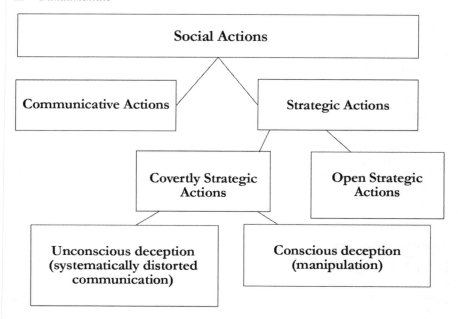

Figure 1.2 Classification of social actions
Source: Habermas (1984).

audiences. The open strategic act is easy to identify—for example, advertising with a visible sender. Hidden strategic action is more difficult to discern. Hidden strategic action ranges from lobbying (direct, sometimes informal, contacts with political decision-makers) and product placement in movies or blogs to media coverage that is initiated and planned by professional sources influencing journalists. This communication process is vertical—that is, the organization speaks to someone following a strategy.

A communicative act is equal and the goal is more participation than efficiency. There are undeniable parallels with Carey's (2009) sensemaking communication perspective, as we discussed earlier. According to this thinking, communication is true to the etymological origin of the word—to share common meaning—and the only goal is for everyone to agree (reach consensus). The communication process is horizontal: different actors talk to each other.

Habermas (1984) has created a formula for an ideal speech situation. This ideal requires that 1) all persons who can speak and act are also able to participate in the discussion and have the same right to express their views, 2) all persons have a right to submit proposals for what is to be discussed, and 3) no person may be prevented from using the rights enumerated by the other items. Habermas's ideal is an objective and rational discussion in which everyone can participate. Decisions are thus made via the consensus that is arrived at, based on an objective and analytical basis.

Dialogues, discussions, and debates

A dialogue is not the same as a discussion. This is the conclusion of one of the leading dialogue researchers, William Isaacs (1999). He has researched organizations and different forms of communication and, like Habermas, has tried to describe the ideal. But Isaacs clearly distinguishes between dialogues, discussions, and debates. He believes that the Western and modern way of communicating through discussion and debate, which may be considered the basis for Habermas's ideals, has become too conflict-oriented. Instead of reaching out to achieve new perceptions, communication follows pre-determined patterns. The solution to this problem is to enhance the ability to listen. Only when we adopt open listening for the purpose of understanding the other or the others do we have a proper (generating) dialogue. The dialogue is based on listening without resistance, reflecting underlying norms and approaches, and then generating new insights, knowledge, and a collective opinion. A constructive discussion is based on trying to argue for and defend what has already been decided. However, by using facts and analysis, a synthesis (of the opposite arguments) can be achieved. A debate is also based on the defense of an already established position, but less through objective analysis and more through rhetorical approaches where the purpose is to win over the other or the others. From a communicative standpoint debates are counter-productive since they lock people into pre-established positions and reinforce what has already been said. Isaacs emphasizes that there are of course places for discussion and debate—for example, in political discourse, when people needs to get a clear idea of what different parties or candidates want to do and which ideology they base their ideas on. But too often we judge the counterparty in advance and do not listen actively. We make interpretations of opinions and express opinions without showing respect to the other and devote most of the time formulating the defense of our own opinions. The discussion may lead to negotiation through compromise, while the goal of dialogue is increased common understanding.

Isaacs', Habermas's and Grunigs' descriptions of dialogue, discussion, and symmetrical communication are relevant to strategic communication. More, they are exciting and work as sources of inspiration. Considering the different models and ideals as achievable formulas may be more doubtful, especially if we assume that no communication situations that are simple and not influenced by history, hierarchies, or rhetorical dimensions.

2   What is strategy?

A large part of the discussion on strategy is based on a traditional and linear view of the concept, which assumes that a certain plan of activities and actions leads to a certain desired effect (Moss, Warnaby, & Newman, 2000). Moss and others also concluded that research about strategy in the management field completely lacks discussions involving strategic communication and public relations dimensions. At the same time, strategy as a dimension in strategic communication and closely related fields has been taken for granted and seen as something rather instrumental and uncomplicated, something that primarily concerns communication managers. However, there are examples of research (Moss, Warnaby, & Thame, 1996) that point out the need to strategically consider communication efforts and programs in order to achieve the overall goals of the organization. Furthermore, there are some examples of researchers who have attempted to integrate strategy research with public relations research, as well as some examples of research in which the science-theoretical basis for public relations strategies is discussed and questioned (Holtzhausen, 2002). We want to argue that the low level of interest and little serious reflection on strategy also applies to practitioners. Communication professionals talk about and carry out strategy continuously, but maybe not always according to a rational logic. One may even ask whether the rational strategy talk really reflects reality—indeed, this constitutes a significant research question for the future. In other words: is there a one-to-one relationship between the fancy strategy success stories told at various conferences or in books and articles and what really happens when strategic communication is enacted? Are the rational stories mainly retrospective and in fact rationalizations of activities and tactics that "just happened", unrelated to strategies and plans?

Strategic theory originates from military theory, a field that is centuries-old. However, a strategic perspective on business, as we embrace it today, emerged in the 1940s, primarily in the United States. Before that there were, of course, theories of leadership and management, which can relate to strategy, but they primarily focused on internal organizational production processes, not markets, environment, or customers and consumption (Knights & Morgan, 1991).

Tactics and strategy

There are two concepts that are common in the management field and also often used in organizations: tactics and strategy. However, the question is what is the actual difference between these two concepts. If we start with tactics, the word comes from the Greek word *taktike*, which means the art of setting up soldiers in a suitable battle scheme. In other words, the word has a military origin and is about reaching a goal by defeating an enemy in a given battle. Transferred to a civil context, tactics involve winning in a competitive situation and refer to the means and approaches used to deal with this. The word strategy also stems from the military. The etymological origin is *strategia*, a Greek word for the art of planning and directing overall military operations in a war or battle, focusing on overall and long-term goals. Strategy is consequently more comprehensive and macro-oriented than tactics and in military contexts is about attaining political goals such as achieving and maintaining peace or changing power relations between two states. The strategy concept has been transferred to a number of different fields, especially within business but also in government, NGOs and the like. Strategy in this context is about where an organization is now and how it can win over other players or adapt to different external and internal forces. Thus, strategy focuses on an organization's comparative benefits and performance (Barney, 2002). The strategy concept has become very common in public organization—e.g. in universities or municipalities. Discussing strategy at seminars and meetings and writing it down in manifestos or plans is a common practice in most organizations. The strategy path can sometimes be compared to therapy—the purpose is to make people feel safe and secure in their own organization. If an organization has a strategy, it is more likely that coworkers and external stakeholders perceive it as professional.

According to traditional theory based on a rationality philosophy (see chapter 4), organizational management, sometimes with the help of external consultants, needs targeted plans that are implemented using particular tactics at lower levels in the organization. Being rational in this context means that, through a careful review of different options, you can choose the optimal option for achieving your overall goals. This means that all available information must be collected and assessed. This is not possible in practice, however, because we humans have limited ability to treat and take stock of the amount of information that would be required to make the optimal and most rational decision. A common starting point for a lot of strategic research is that the top management of an organization is adequately qualified and informed to make important strategic decisions Wilson and Jarzabkowski (2004). Furthermore, good strategies are supposed to be based on background research and need to be implemented top-down. Communication professionals are one group out of many in an organization that have their own methods for collecting background material. For communication professionals, benchmark analysis (comparing different positions), media analysis (focusing on media image and coverage), and quantitative surveys (searching for attitudes among stakeholders towards the organization) are typical tools. Communication professionals talk about four different steps to optimize strategic communication: survey, planning, implementation, and evaluation Mintzberg and Westley, 2001; cf. Wilson and Jarzabkowski, 2004). It is often assumed that if these four steps are followed, you work strategically, which implicitly suggests that you are more effective than those who "only" work tactically. Those who work strategically are thus seen as proactive, while tacticians are called reactive. The fact that this division and view are so widespread is not strange considering that so many textbooks (Vargo & Lusch, 2004; Wilson, 2000), university programs, and consultants preach strategic planning according to a rational logic. James Grunig's (Grunig & Hunt, 1984; Grunig & Repper, 1992) well-known public relations models are based on a rational strategic logic, as are many of the best-practice descriptions contained in consultancy books (so-called airport management literature, since they are often sold at airports). Public relations literature often refers to two types of communication professionals: strategists and technicians (e.g. Broom, 1982; Broom & Dozier, 1986; Dozier, 1992). In practical work this division is diffused. A competent strategist must also know about and be able for the craft and work involved with practical questions in order to work strategically and for the long term.

Strategic schools and strategic perspectives

There is a lot of research on strategy, especially in the organization and management fields. It must be noted that there is no consensus or generally accepted definition of strategy (Chaffee, 1985; Mintzberg, 1973). One reason for this is that strategy contains many dimensions and is dependent on situations and contexts. Strategy is usually perceived as something palpable or a thing. This means that strategy is seen as something that an organization *has*, such as a communication strategy. Contemporary strategy researchers (e.g. Jarzabkowski & Whittington, 2008a; Johnson, Melin, & Whittington, 2003) are critical of the traditional perception of strategy and point out that strategy is instead something human beings *do*—activities conducted by organizational members. The late modern approach to strategy means that strategy is not an organization's property but rather a way of working. Consequently, strategy is a social practice—that is, an organized human activity (Schatzki, 2005) and not something that is solely linked to an organization's activities.

In strategy research, there is a historical divide between "content" and "process" approaches. It is possible to compare these two approaches with the transmission or ritual approaches to communication described in the previous chapter. The content approach puts the type of strategy at the center, while the process approach focuses on strategy formulation and implementation (Whittington, 2007) and is devoted to how and why things evolve over time. Researchers who follow the process approach are critical of the idea of fixed strategies and instead focus on investigating what happens when strategy, organizations, and individuals "collide" (Wilson & Jarzabkowski, 2004). Strategy process researchers believe that strategy should not be understood as linear or as something that happens when a long period of thinking is followed by a long period of action. Instead, these activities interrelate and are mutually dependent.

Strategy as a research field can be dated to the early 1960s, with pioneers like Ackoff, Ansoff, Drucker, and Selznick representing the process school and Chandler and Porter representing the content school. In the mid-1950s, Peter Drucker (1955) launched the concept of management by objectives (MBO), which was of major importance for corporate strategy work. According to Drucker, work on setting goals, and efforts to achieve these, should occur at all hierarchical levels of an organization. Two years later, Philip Selznick (1957) introduced the well-known SWOT analysis, the acronym standing for strengths, weaknesses, opportunities, and threats. The analysis is based on the matching and comparing of internal factors with external factors and the development of a strategy based on the outcome. The SWOT analysis is still used in many organizations. Alfred Chandler (1962) pointed out that organizations must create long-term strategies to achieve clear structure and governance and a clear business focus. Three years later, Igor Ansoff (1965) introduced gap analysis in the strategy field. The idea was that organizations should analyze the current situation and the desired future situation and build a strategy that reduces the gap between them. Russell Ackoff (1970) contributed a system-oriented overall approach to strategic planning. In 1980, the well-known researcher Michael E. Porter published *Competitive Strategy*, in which he emphasizes that the purpose of a business strategy is to strengthen an organization's competitiveness.

Over the years, various strategy schools have evolved, emphasizing different aspects of strategy. Henry Mintzberg and Joseph Lampel (1999) have mapped ten different schools, three of which are normative and seven descriptive. In an attempt to describe the development of research on strategy, Mintzberg and Lampel (1999) concluded that "We are the blind people and strategy formation is our elephant. Each of us, in trying to cope with the mysteries of the beast, grabs hold of some part or other" (p. 21). Mintzberg and Lampel mean that the different schools must open up to each other and acknowledge the strengths and weaknesses of each school. This broader perspective, they believe, will allow the elephant (strategy) to be better understood. Mintzberg (1973) and Chaffee (1985) have attempted to capture what the broad research on strategy says. The starting point for researchers trying to reconcile different schools is neo-positivistic—it is assumed that a true reality exists "out there". Researchers based on a social constructionist perspective do not try to find common ground or combine different perspectives. Rather, they believe that each perspective can give us a certain picture and understanding and it is enriching for research that researchers do not agree (see Deetz, 2000, and his corresponding discussion on perspectives in organizational communication).

Whittington's typology of strategies

In this chapter we have chosen to use Richard Whittington's (2001) typology to present different perspectives in strategic research. Whittington is one of the leading researchers in the field of strategy and we believe this typology describes the different orientations in a particularly useful way. Whittington has identified four different perspectives on strategy in both theory and practice. In this context, it may be appropriate to point out that his typology concerns so-called ideal models—that is, properties and characteristics are clearer than in reality, where they easily get mixed. Whittington does not link the discussions on strategies with strategic communication or communication strategies, but we have added this dimension.

Classical strategy

The first perspective is the traditional classical strategy model, which has much in common with the original etymological meaning of strategy. As noted above, the classic perspective is based on a high level of confidence in rationality at all levels of a system. This was a common way of understanding organizations in the United States in the 1960s (Whittington, 2004). A human being is seen as a rational creature, following the same logic the father of economics, Adam Smith, used when he described "economic man". It is assumed that all humans are highly calculating and utility-maximizing. Furthermore, it is assumed that causes and effects can be fully controlled. In order to achieve optimal effects, those with greatest responsibility in an organization must create planning features that affect all decisions. Harvard professor Michael E. Porter (see, for example, Porter, 1980) is one prominent researcher in this tradition. In practice, the classical strategy is very rare; few organizations fully work according to it (Mintzberg & Westley, 2001). The ideal model for the traditional strategy is found in military organizations, in major manufacturing industries, and in large public organizations. The management perspective is internal and information is analyzed in chronological steps (first this happens, then this, and so on). Within research, as described above, the first strategy researchers belong to the classical strategy perspective, but they have been criticized since the 1960s. The classical perspective of strategy can also be found in introductory books for strategic communication and public relations. Students will learn that they need to follow different logical steps as they develop a strategy. First, a certain type of communication problem should be identified and analyzed using a general strategy model borrowed from the management field, such as the SWOT analysis. Different action options are then analyzed and a number of different options are set. In the next step, tactics (activities) are produced—for example, media campaigns or internal meetings with the employees. Implementation is then considered to be complete and evaluations are carried out, primarily using quantitative surveys. Ideally, the entire process follows a linear, detailed written plan.

Deviations from the plan are not accepted and risk creating a crisis in the communications department. Practitioners generally have great skill in planning and develop significant competence in writing documents (policies, plans, etc.) and conducting surveys, but they are usually unprepared for creative improvisation—situational acting is neglected. In other words, there is a strong risk that the plan will be followed even if unforeseen events occur during the process (see Czarniawska, 2008). If there is criticism of the tactical implementation of the plan, the communication professionals will find it difficult to change it and instead will defend it. The view of communication that dominates the classical perspective is the transmission view (Carey, 2009).

The classical perspective of strategy is primarily found in large organizations. Furthermore, it is likely that this perspective is more common in organizations where the communication department is based at the headquarters, far from the micro-places in the organization where value is created through services and products (see, for example, Falkheimer & Heide, 2010; Hübner, 2007).

Evolutionary perspective

The evolutionary perspective of strategy is diametrically different from the classical perspective, especially from a communicative viewpoint. Whittington has chosen to call this perspective evolutionary, but it could also be named a Darwinist perspective. A starting point is that there is no need to put too many resources into trying to predict or control organizations' environment or markets. The effectiveness of a rational but uncontrolled market is fundamental and leadership, strategies, and plans have no causal significance for organizational success. The question then becomes what method is preferable from this perspective. The most common is product or service differentiation by producing and distributing different customer offerings. The logical basis for this method is simply that it is the only possible one, since only an uncontrolled market can reveal what works and does not work. According to the evolutionary perspective, there is also reason to minimize administrative functions in organizations, since few plans and strategies have any real value. According to the same logic, organizations must deliver new products and services at high speed, and if they are not successful, they must be withdrawn from the market very quickly. This is an approach that is common in popular culture. New artists, magazines, and television shows usually have a short life if they do not meet the financial requirements of the owners.

From a strategic communication perspective, the role of communication in the evolutionary strategy is very simple—the aim is to maximize publicity and attention during the launch of new solutions, products, and services. In practice this means that strategic communication is used as a sub-discipline of marketing communications. The ideal practitioner might be a marketing professional or a former journalist who receives editorial publishing on behalf of his or her clients. This form of attention seeking is sometimes seen as belonging to the past, but the evolutionary strategy perspective is used in many modern organizations, especially those offering low-income products and services. Examples of such products and services are toilet paper, salt, flour, and train tickets. The evolutionary perspective is also based on the transmission view of communication, with a high degree of confidence in direct effects on major target groups.

The processual perspective

The third perspective is the processual perspective. It could also be called the sensemaking or relativistic perspective because it challenges the rationality of organizations and their stakeholders. The epistemology (i.e. the view of what knowledge is and how it is produced) is social constructionism, which focuses on how sensemaking processes relate to the social context in which they are communicated. In other words, communication is not a transmission process between a transmitter and a receiver, but a process where participants construct meaning when they talk and share messages. In the processual strategic perspective, leadership and plans are not dismissed, but the rational basis for strategy is understood in a completely different way. The ontological approach (ontology—how the world is represented) argues that reality should be interpreted as dependent on chaotic contexts that are impossible to describe in terms of simple cause-and-effect perspectives. Because organizations are extremely fluid and constantly changing, strategists cannot predict the future. However, strategy has an important role in organizational meaning making or collective therapy. If strategies are created through optimal interaction and are decentralized, they can lead to increased motivation and gather organizational members around certain goals.

Overall, processual strategy researchers agree that strategies are of primary importance for internal work. First, they are important for coherent and integrated organizational learning and for creating a sense of security among organization members (Weick, 1979). If an organization is to achieve these positive goals, the strategies must be flexible, open, and adapted to the local situation and practice. Furthermore, the strategies must be comprehensive and not too detailed or they risk locking the organization into certain actions.

From a strategic communication perspective, the processual perspective means that traditional ways of working with communication processes must be questioned. For example, when detailed communication strategies are created, external consultants are often hired. They tend to work with standard models that do not consider the specific context since they have no experience of this context. The processual perspective also questions the boundaries between internal and external communication and proposes an integrated and holistic approach. Using this perspective in practice is not very difficult because the whole theory is based on what really happens in the lives of organizations. That is, even if leaders and communication professionals say they work according to the traditional perspective, the processual perspective is what they really use—how they improvise and make sense of events retrospectively. Mintzberg and Westley (2001) describe the relationship between thinking and action as follows: "Successful people know that when they are stuck, they must experiment. Thinking may drive doing, but doing just as surely drives thinking. We don't just think in order to act, we act in order to think" (p. 91).

In order to learn new things, one has to experiment and test new solutions to problems. In practice, the processual perspective implies that communication professionals should focus more on the pedagogical aspects of the profession and create communicative spaces for formal and informal communication with the aim of enhancing the reflection and learning of organizational members.

The system perspective

The system perspective is partly related to the process perspective because it shares its foundation in social psychology and sociology. The system perspective—which involves adapting to different system logics through symmetrical communication or other models—is well known in public relations. In strategy research, system theory leads to the conclusion that leadership and decision-making are crucial and planning and change strategies are less important. System theory is a large and complex field with different orientations that are difficult to summarize. In this context, the main argument in system theory is that it is not possible to distinguish an organization from its environment. Organizations are dependent on changes in their environment but also affect their environment. From a strategic perspective, the main purpose is to create methods and structures that enable the organization to deal with this mutual dependence and adapt to its social and cultural context. In other words, the success of an organization depends on how well it adapts to other social systems. Some conclusions are similar to those associated with the processual perspective—for example, that there are no universal strategies or models that work. However, there is a crucial difference: the system perspective does not take into account the interpretations of or meanings created by organizational members on a micro level, but focuses on the macro level.

From a strategic communication perspective, the system theory questions the demand for a universal model (for example, a general return on investment model). The strong emergence of strategic communication as an industry and organizational function in many countries over the last decades could be explained using system theory as a method for different systems of dealing with entropy (the degree of disorder or chaos). Consequently, it means that strategic communication is used as a solution to complex organizational problems: creating order in chaos through information. If communication is to act as a strategic resource, this system needs to be complex. According to the classical perspective, simple strategic thinking will not solve the problem.

In practice, the system perspective is probably quite common. Communication professionals are tasked with adapting organizations' activities and representation to the prevailing standards, values, and culture of the surrounding systems.

Summary of perspectives

In Table 2.1 below, we have tried to clarify the differences between perspectives by highlighting seven different characteristics: strategy, purpose, communicative focus, administrative role for strategic communication, processes, feedback, and epistemology.

Practical use in strategic communication

In this section we continue to develop the reasoning related to the third perspective, the processual, focusing on its potential value for strategic communication. There has long been process- and practice-oriented thinking in the management field, and so it is with strategic communication. Generally speaking, traditional research within the strategy field tends to stay at a macro level, with a fair degree of separation from the actual practice of strategies where they are introduced and used. However, recently, organizational actions and interactions have been re-highlighted in research (Jarzabkowski, 2004; Jarzabkowski, Balogun, & Seidl, 2007; Whittington, 2006, 2007; Wilson & Jarzabkowski, 2004). This development is part of a general trend in the social sciences moving away from normative models that are often too simplistic. The development has various names, such as practice use (Orlikowski, 1992;

Table 2.1 Four perspectives on strategic communication strategy inspired by Whittington (2001)

	Classical	*Evolutionary*	*Process*	*System*
Strategy	Rationality	Efficiency	Skill	Adaptation
Purpose	Promote long-term planning	Support exposure on the market	Supporting sensemaking processes	Map adjustments to social systems
Communicative focus	Internal	External	Internal	External
Administrative role of strategic communication	A centralized function with clear borders to other functions	A publicity focus as part of the marketing function	Decentralized, support of processes at all levels, close to the local meetings	Integrated in management at the highest level
Processes	Investigating (weak relation to the implementation)	Darwinistic (survival of the fittest and fastest)	Negotiation on a local (micro) level	Analytical at a macro level
Feedback	Documents and plans	Visibility	Local understanding	Adjustments of the system
Epistemology (dominating)	Positivism	Positivism	Social constructionism	Social constructionism

Orr, 1996) and linguistic turn (Alvesson & Kärreman, 2000b, 2011a), and can also be seen as part of more human management and organizational research (Weick, 1979). Based on Weick's reasoning for "organizing" (as a continuous process) instead of "organization", Johnson, Melin, and Whittington (2003) suggest a greater focus on micro strategy work. This emphasizes the strategy activities—that is, what members of the organization *do* with the strategy. This means that researchers' interest should be directed not only at the formal development of strategies at management level but also at the strategy practitioners, who are often organizational executives (see Whittington, 2004). Similar criticism has been expressed by Jarzabkowski (2004), who concludes that there is a gap between the theory of what members of the organization say they do and what they really do in everyday organizational life. Jarzabkowski uses the concept of strategy-as-practice to illustrate the relationship between individual micro-practice (i.e. their daily work) and macro-practice in terms of norms and values. This focuses on the normative and economically dominated theory of strategy research and avoids simplified ideas about how senior executives work (Jarzabkowski & Whittington, 2008b). According to Jarzabkowski, Balogun and Seidl (2007), strategy is "a particular type of activity that is connected with particular practices, such as strategic planning, annual reviews, strategy workshops and their associated discourses" (p. 9).

Based on the perception that strategy is something that organizers create, make, and realize rather than something an organization has, Marchiori and Bulgacov (2012) argue that we must understand the importance of communication in the creation of strategies. Strategy is thus a communicative practice that is conducted at different levels in an organization wherein the organization is continuously created and reproduced (see more in the introductory chapter). In everyday life, organizational members create and modify strategies by interpreting events and giving meaning to them as well as interacting with others.

Wilson and Jarzabkowski (2004) emphasize that there is always a reciprocal relationship between macro and micro. Micro-level activities have macro effects, while those activities are influenced by macro-phenomena connected to political, social, and economic institutions (for example, industry standards and governmental policies).

As mentioned above, reflections on strategy as concept and practice have been too often absent in research on strategic communication. We therefore argue for a turn where researchers pay attention to the communication professionals practices, based on the processual perspective of strategy—that is, what practitioners do when they act as communication professionals in organizations. Such research could be carried out using ethnographic methods such as shadowing practitioners and observing different activities (Alvesson & Kärreman, 2011b; Nothhaft, 2010). Furthermore, we would like to propose a more reflexive epistemological approach to research—that is, we would like to see researchers taking more inspiration from social constructionism, which has achieved recognition in other social science research fields.

Generally speaking, people have a rather negative image of strategic communications, and especially public relations—they regard it as propaganda activity aimed at influencing individuals in a certain direction (e.g. their opinions or actions) (cf. Cheney & Christensen, 2006; Coombs & Holladay, 2007). Even in the academic world, public relations have relatively low status, which is probably linked to the fact that the majority of theories in public relations are based on a functionalist perspective (see Holtzhausen, 2002; Holtzhausen, 2012; Toth, 2002). Researchers like Cheney and Christensen (2001b) have criticized public relations as an academic field, saying that "public relations ought to become even more intellectually expansive, more critically reflective, and more cognizant of the diverse forms of organizational activity in today's world" (p. 179).

Public relations appear to be cemented in a traditional epistemology and there is a clear need for new perspectives and epistemologies to enable the field to evolve and raise its status and social significance. McKie (2001) emphasizes that public relations researchers need to be more open to research in other fields and thereby gain inspiration for alternative ways of understanding different phenomena.

Regarding communication professionals' attitude to communication strategies, they would seem to be rather unproblematic phenomena seen from a traditional classical perspective. Communication is understood according to the transmission view on communication. This means that communication is perceived as transferring information through any medium from a sender to a particular recipient, who is supposed to "open the package" in order to understand the message (Axley, 1984; Varey, 2000). The challenge for communication professionals is to identify a target group, choose the correct words to convey a given meaning, select the appropriate medium, and start the transfer process of information to the recipients. Similarly, strategies are planned and implemented in accordance with the classical perspective of strategy, meaning that everything can be understood and planned with "correct" and sufficient information.

Consequences for communication practice

"Plans are nothing; planning is everything" is a well-known axiom formulated by former American president (1953–1961) Dwight D. Eisenhower. It describes in a useful way a mindset that is crucial in an ever-changing and complex world. It is not possible to face a chaotic world with pre-programmed processes. Instead, organizations must develop the capacity to look into the chaos while developing the ability to improvise in order to handle different situations.

In the mid-1970s, several researchers stressed that organizations should not be understood as closely linked systems, as per the classic view of strategy. In organizations that are closely linked systems, behaviors, and actions are closely related through carefully designed tasks, descriptions, coordination, and control mechanisms. A problem with this rather common perception of organizations as rational units is that it is not realistic. In reality, things and actions are not rationally coordinated and controlled—plans are not followed in detail, decision-making is delegated, coordination fails, and control and follow-up are not absolute or complete. A clear advantage of a loosely linked system is that an organization has more opportunity to perceive changes inside and outside the system. This can be explained by the sand metaphor: sand as a medium is more sensitive to change than a stone block and is thus better suited to perceive the wind's shifts.

In our research on strategy-in-practice we have found that communication professionals working closely with events—for example, at the forefront of organizations—tend to use long-term and overall plans (e.g. Falkheimer & Heide, 2006). They seem to improvise in order to adapt quickly to a fluid and ever-changing world. With rigid plans there is a high risk of action paralysis or delayed reaction, as plans are read and followed. In leadership research, improvisation has increasingly been highlighted as key to success. In contrast to improvisation, traditional strategy thinking takes it for granted that rational decisions based on a large amount of information are possible to achieve. But as the Nobel laureate Herbert Simon (1947) has taught us: it is only possible to achieve bounded rationality.

Concluding reflections

Is communication strategy thus something that relates only to the communications manager and the CEO? Our answer to that question is of course a resounding *no*. On the contrary, strategy-in-practice concerns and involves a large number of organizational members at different levels of an organization. Many times, and in different contexts involving both practitioners and researchers, the need for communication heads to be members of management appears the only way to achieve legitimacy and institutionalization. However, we do not think that communication professionals being given a leading role is any sort of panacea or universal model.

We are convinced that communication professionals may only show their true value to an organization by leaving their ivory tower and discontinuing the megaphone function of delivering the voice of management to various functions. Rather, communication professionals should begin to act as internal communication consultants (Heide & Simonsson, 2011; Zerfass & Franke, 2013). The real value that communication professionals can contribute will be confirmed when they begin working within actual work processes in the organization and support and help managers with different levels of communication and communication matters. For example, when it comes to the development of innovation in organizations, managers have an underlying responsibility to encourage discussions and interactions that can lead to new advances. Managers therefore have both the opportunity and the responsibility to act as communication promoters, backed by the active support and assistance of communication professionals (Zerfass & Huck, 2007).

3 What is strategic communication?

Strategic communication has emerged as a professional and academic concept during the last two decades. Strategic communication is today a term used by executives, managers, politicians, diplomats, communication professionals, public relations and communication consultants, military officers, and several other professional groups. Strategic communication has also become established within university and higher education, with an increasing number of departments all over the world offering courses and undergraduate and graduate programs with a specialization in strategic communication. Despite this development in practice and in academia there is great confusion over what strategic communication actually means and what it is. This is not strange given the relative newness of the concept, and similar to definitional debates in other academic fields and disciplines. A Google search using the key words "strategic communication" in December 2017 generated in unbelievable 18 500 000 hits! If one restricts the review of the hits to the first hundred, a clear pattern is detectable. Most of the links point to university courses or to professional agencies that offer services in the field. Many times, strategic communication seems to refer to planned communication, communication campaigns, or tactical public relations. An example of this campaign perspective on strategic communication is shown below.

> Strategic communication is the purposeful communication by a person or an organization designed to persuade audiences with the goal of increasing knowledge, changing attitudes, or inducing desired behavior. Strategic communication campaigns are generally designed to respond to the perceived communications needs of significant publics.
>
> (Connolly-Ahern, 2008, p. 765)

But planned communication is not the same thing as strategic communication. Planned communication is tactical communication, typically a communication activity to gain more customers or make some target group change its behavior or attitudes (Windahl & Signitzer, 2009). In other words, planned communication is not related to the overall goal of an organization, but rather to tactical goals at a mid-range level, such as the sale of products or services or getting citizens involved in taking care of newly arrived refugees in a municipality. Planned communication is often based on a traditional one-way communication mindset in which a sender takes the initiative in the communication process and is assumed to be the one that has control over the situation. Planned communication has a clear relation to some of the mass communication theories mentioned before, viewing human beings as passive individuals who are possible to control, direct, and persuade—at least if the communication professional has the "right" tools, media, and message. Many of the consultancy agencies that use the concept strategic communication do so because it sounds trendy or elegant, when the actual activity on offer is planned communication. This is not only true for strategic communication. Other professional groups show the same tendency: by using what is seen as a classier or more glamorous concept, professionals hope that their status will be enhanced (see Alvesson, 2013).

Based on fundamental published research by established scholars, we define strategic communication as conscious communication activities aimed at reaching overall organizational goals (Falkheimer & Heide, 2011a). Hence, it is not the goals of a certain communication activity that are at the center, but overall and long-term goals. Strategic communication builds on an understanding of the fundamental importance of communication for the existence, legitimacy, and operations of an organization. In other words, communication is not only viewed as a tool for the distribution of information or a tool to facilitate conversations between organizational members.

Strategic communication appears to embrace many things. In this chapter we will further review different understandings of the concept and describe our own understanding.

Definition of strategic communication

Strategic communication can be defined as the study of how organizations use communication purposefully to fulfill their overall missions (Frandsen & Johansen, 2017).

The traditional research fields

There are at least three separate research fields, mainly developed after the Second World War, which focus on different aspects of organizations' goal-oriented communication: public relations, organizational communication, and marketing communication. Since the establishment of these fields, various different approaches and perspective groups have emerged. Contemporary research studies within the three fields have more in common than ever before due to social, cultural, and political-economic developments. Common goals for organizations' communication include the production of understanding, durable relations, and a common identity. In strategic communication the three traditional fields are integrated into one framework. One reason for this is that it is considered that internal and external communication are interconnected. Below follows a short discussion of each of the three traditional research fields.

Public relations

The field of modern public relations has its origins in both the US and Europe. In the US there is an obvious relationship to the establishment of modern mass media, the growth of large companies, political communication, and public opinion formation related to the wars of the last century (Ewen, 1996). During the first decades of the twentieth century, public relations in most cases was used for so-called damage control (crisis and reputation management), operated by press agents who worked with defending organizations during different types of crisis. The historical foundation of US public relations may, according to critical research, be related to a conservative understanding of so-called mass society, where public relations was a tool used by the elite to control and manipulate public opinion, which was viewed as irrational and dangerous (Bernays, 1955). In other parts of the world, for example Great Britain and Sweden, the historical development of public relations was more related to the public sector (including the military sector) and viewed as a tool to inform, educate, and persuade citizens to think and behave according to different policies (Larsson, 2005). Research within public relations as a discipline is relatively young. Even if it is possible to relate public relations to early research on rhetoric, opinion formation, and mass communication, the main research paradigm emerged with James Grunig and his colleagues' empirical Excellence project in the 1980s.

Public relations has been defined in hundreds of ways. Most of the definitions maintain that public relations is a management function that aims to produce and preserve good relations between an organization and its different publics. In the introduction to *Handbook of Public Relations,* the editor Robert Heath (2010) writes that there are two diametrically different perspectives on public relations. On the one side, public relations is understood as a management instrument that only serves the interest of an organization; on the other side, public relations is understood as something that serves the interests of society by listening to different publics and increasing their influence over organizational activities. The research that has grown in strength is based on the societal approach, not only focusing on organizational interests. According to Heath (2010), and we share his view:

> Those of us interested in issues, rhetoric dialogue, and discourse continue to emphasize that information does not serve for much without interpretation and advocacy, however loud and subtle. We lose sight of the richness of dialogue if we only feature information and don't address how meaning is crafted, shared, and enacted in ways that relate to collective and competitive sense making of the information/fact and evaluations at play.
>
> (s. xii)

Heath claims that it is important to consider and reflect on the logical fundament of public relations—the basic aim. The traditional publicity perspective (with its focus on mass media) limits the scope of public relations by exclusively focusing on message formulation and the transmission of information in order to get attention, convince, and persuade. With the new perspective, mutual relations with different publics is what an organization needs in order to be successful in the long run. An assumption with this perspective is that publics such as unions, the media, governmental institutions, and activist groups that have established a good relationship with an organization will probably not act against it or hurt it. Another assumption is that if there are good relations and continuing dialogue, issues will never become critical. Emerging issues are handled in a continuous interaction between the publics and the organization.

The foremost guru within the public relations field, James E. Grunig (2001)—whose models were described in Chapter 2—holds that qualitative communication is key to rewarding relations. According to Grunig, communication should be symmetrical—that is, communication should be a dialogue between two equal partners where both try to understand the other's argument and are willing to reconsider their original position. Grunig builds his thinking on system theory and the goal is to achieve a good balance (preferably to reach a "win-win" position) between the interests of the organization and those of the public. As mentioned before, the symmetrical PR model has been heavily criticized since it means that organizations must constantly adapt to the ethical preferences of the various publics. In response to this critique, Dozier, Grunig, and Grunig (1995) developed the mixed-motive model, in which both asymmetrical and symmetrical communication can be used to, as appropriate, convince publics or adapt the business to their wishes. PR practitioners should, according to Grunig et al., act as the ears and eyes of the management and in a middleman role between the organization and its publics, with the aim of helping them understand each other's interests.

The Grunigs' PR theories do not provide much information on how practitioners should act to become good spokespersons of the organizations. PR researchers have therefore consulted classical rhetorical principles to better explain how practitioners act and which tactics may be used to reach a harmonious accord between organization and public (Heath, 2001). The rhetoric is dialogic and each participant should try to convince others of the superiority of their argument. In other words, one should not stick to a particular view once faced with a better, more rational, argument.

Rhetoric reminds us that everything an organization does or says will be interpreted by a public or publics. It is thus fundamentally important that communication professionals try to map facts, values, and policies that can assist organizations build mutually rewarding communities. The quality of communities depends on how organizations relate to them—whether they try to dominate them or cooperate with them, whether they communicate *with* them or *to* them (Starck & Kruckeberg, 2001). Few of us believe that building relations with different communities is a simple process. Researchers often claim that the key to success in work with communities is dialogue and seeing each community as unique and with special interests. Without this it is difficult to reach any meaningful relationship.

Since the beginning of the twenty-first century research in public relations has been taking new forms, increasingly departing from a strict focus on organizations and embracing perspectives that analyze public relations as a societal or sociological phenomenon (Ihlen, Fredrikson, & Ruler, 2009). Some researchers (e.g. Wehmeier and Winkler, 2013) try to break the theoretical isolation that public relations in general have locked into by connecting public relations with other fields such as organizational communication. This also means that more critical and reflexive research has evolved—for instance, focusing on public relations as a symbolic power tool that can be used by bodies other than companies or governments (Holtzhausen, 2012).

Organizational communication

The border between public relations and marketing communication is especially unclear when it comes to the field of organizational communication. As a concept, organizational communication is useful as an umbrella notion for all forms of an organization's communication activity. Thus, it could also function as a generic term for both public relations and marketing communication. However, this suggestion could never be realized in practice. Although they all have existed as practice since the beginning of the last century, the three research fields were developed during the 1950s in the US and in different academic departments and faculties. Hence, from the start they have had different interests and aims. The retention of these borders can be explained by academic politics, by academics' desire to maintain their closed fields of interest.

In scientific contexts, organizational communication can be traced back to the 1920s and the Dale Carnegie Institute, whose programs include training managers in rhetoric to help them become more effective communicators. The field was originally called business and industrial communication. Chester Barnard's (1938/1968) book *The Functions of the Executive* and Alexander Heron's (1942) book *Sharing Information with Employees* are considered important milestones; they were the first within the organizational communication research field. During the 1960s organizational communication grew and was established as a modern field by Charles Redding (Redding & Sanborn, 1964), who is considered the founding father. Redding contributed a more scientific approach. He abandoned the traditional transmission view of communication that was dominant within the subject of "speech" and developed a more receiver-oriented view.

Organizational communication is a very wide research field, but Gerald Goldhaber (1993) has found three characteristics. The first characteristic is the starting point: that organizational communication occurs within a complex and open system, which means that it influences and is influenced by the internal and external environment. The second characteristic is that organizational communication involves messages and their flow, aim, direction, and medium. The third characteristic is that organizational communication involves human beings and their attitudes, emotions, relationships, and skills.

Traditionally, organizational communication has focused exclusively on internal communication—the communication between managers and coworkers and between coworkers (Heide et al., 2012). But gradually, as researchers have abandoned the functionalistic perspective on organizations as "boxes" with humans, interest has shifted to close, mutual relationships and the interdependence of internal and external communication.

We agree with Stanley Deetz' (2001) criticism of researchers' aspiration to capture the core of organizational communication. Deetz means that it is far more interesting to reflect on what you perceive, understand, and can do in relation to the different perspectives on organizational communication. In an overview of organizational communication as a research field, Deetz found three comprehensive approaches. In the first approach, organizational communication is seen as a *special field*—something that persons with a formal education in communication have as a profession; this might include communication officers and communication consultants. In the second approach, organizational communication is understood as a certain *phenomenon*—something that exists in organizations. This is probably the most usual understanding of organizational communication, and the one that is most frequently referred to in textbooks within the field. The emphasis here is investigating what could be considered organizational communication and what is something else, how it can be categorized, which factors influence organizational communication such as hierarchy, organizational form, culture, and power and which theories best explain the phenomenon. In the third approach, organizational communication is perceived as a *specific way to describe, explain, and understand* organizations and their business. This implies that researchers from a communication theoretical perspective can explain organizational processes. This is the approach that we find most attractive, since it points out what communication researchers can uniquely contribute to organizational studies. With the first and second approaches, researchers in other subjects such as sociology, philosophy, business administration, and psychology could also conduct studies in organizational communication. This is not per se something negative, but we would like to underline the importance of starting from a solid communication theoretical point of departure when analyzing a communicative perspective on organizational processes.

Marketing communication

In an ever-changing world, where consumers' preferences change in an unpredictable way and where there is massive global competition from other organizations, marketing communication has gradually altered (de

Pelsmacker, Geuens, & van den Bergh, 2010). The modern consumer has a harder and harder task to differentiate between different products and services. For example, it is difficult to discern sneaker quality differences in brands such as Acne, Converse, Lacoste, Le Coq Sportif, or Puma. Further, it is not very difficult for competitors to copy each other's products. The increasing possibility of communicating with consumers through digital media makes it even more difficult to get through the noise with a message to increasingly sophisticated, aware, and skeptical consumer groups (Schultz, 2005). These market conditions have led to greater interest in branding and consumer culture to distinguish different products and services, as well as a widening of the marketing communication field to public relations, digital technologies, and brain research.

Research in marketing communication started at the beginning of the twentieth century, but it was not until the 1950s that empirical research took off (Dahlén, Lange, & Smith, 2010). There is a clear parallel, and related development, in research about mass media and social psychology, which have had significant influence on the development of marketing communication—for example, research on social influence, attitude change, and communication processes.

According to the classical marketing theory, the role of communication is to inform, persuade, and enhance and differentiate choices for consumers. The basic idea is that there should be a process of exchange or transaction of products, services, and values. Traditional marketing is based on Robert J. Lavidge and Gary A. Steiner's (1961) model, *hierarchy of effects.* In this model, consumers move from being aware of a product offered by an organization to having knowledge of it, to liking it and preferring it to other competing products, and finally to being completely convinced of the product's advantages, which will lead to a purchasing decision. The first doctrine in marketing—*the transaction perspective* —was based on the assumption that it was the exchange of money for products and services that was key. Hence, marketing communication was focused on achieving more exchange situations in order to get customers to buy more. Transaction marketing, based on economics, means in practice that organizations disseminate information about their offerings to customers, who are expected to make independent choices from among several competing options (Grönroos, 2015). Customers are more or less perceived as opponents of the organization who with good enough arguments can be persuaded to buy a product.

In the early 1980s a new model for marketing emerged, which focused on cooperation between organization and customers. The cooperation can be short or long, but it is always a buying situation. The new model—*the relational perspective on marketing*—emphasized that the most important aspect of marketing is not the exchange situation, when a customer receives a product or service, but the *value exchange* that takes place (Grönroos, 2015). The understanding is that if good relations can be initiated and maintained, it is more likely that customers will return and buy even more. Value is defined as the customers' experience of a purchase. In other words, value is an immaterial phenomenon that emerges from the relationship between customer and product/service and customer and salesperson. With this marketing perspective there is a certain degree of interdependence and cooperation between the customer and the organization. The customer is in this perspective understood as a resource that, together with the organization, can create the value the customer requests (Grönroos, 2015).

As a research field, marketing communication has developed from short-term tactical campaign communication to interactive, strategic, and relationship-building communication. As part of this development, Joseph Jaffe (2007) introduced the concept *conversational marketing*, which means that consumers should not be regarded as passive, empty containers (spoken *to*), but rather as active interpreters that organizations need to have a dialogue with in order to build and maintain a long relationship (talked *with*). Opportunities to maintain a "dialogue" with customers and engage them has naturally increased significantly with websites and social media. It should also be noted that marketing communication today is largely a question of creating and maintaining high brand value (brand equity).

With increased *servicification*, traditional principles of business management, based on detailed control of production companies, are no longer valid and new principles for the management of companies are required. The concept of service management was used increasingly in the 1990s by marketing researchers, although the term was first coined in the 1980s (Normann, 1984). Service management can be seen as leadership principles that guide decisions and leadership in service competition. Advocates of service management believe that the management of all business functions must be focused on the customer and the service value they produce. This means that marketing thinking should not be confined to the marketing department but involve the whole organization—in other words, market-oriented rather than traditional production-oriented business management. According to this thinking, products companies (e.g. car companies) may also be viewed as service organizations requiring different forms of service in the areas of delivery, installation, and complaint handling (Grönroos, 2015). The old transaction and product approach to marketing is no longer valid because the relationship with the customer does not end when he or she has purchased the product. The modern view of marketing is that it is not isolated to one department performing special operations with certain tools and methods, but rather that it is a way of thinking that should imbue the entire organization. The ideas of service management have a lot in common with the ideas behind strategic communication.

Service management contributes an increased interest in and a shift toward producing good, long-term customer relationships (Grönroos, 2015). Further, service management implies a shift of focus from internal to external consequences and paying more interest to processes rather than organizational structures. This is meant to improve the opportunities for the organization to adapt to changes in the environment, such as changing customer preferences and needs. The same argument is valid internally. If the emphasis is on structure, there is an risk that an organization becomes centralized and that the fixed structures have a negative impact on horizontal communication between the employees and between the different departments. Thus, important informal communication tends to become ignored. This is problematic since this form of communication creates new ideas, thoughts can be tested and valued, and information and knowledge that can be shared within the organization.

An ambition to break traditional borders

We have previously underlined that the boundaries between the different research fields that are interested in organizations' communication (i.e. marketing communication, organizational communication, and public relations) are unclear. The reason is that "internal" communication does not stay in the organization but also reaches out to other stakeholders, and "external" communication (e.g. marketing communication and advertising) also reaches employees and has a potential impact on them. Additionally, there is mutual interdependence between internal and external communication. Few organizations have been successful with their brand communications to external stakeholders when employees do not accept what the brand stands for; employees are the most important ambassadors of an organization and can materialize the brand values in their meetings with clients. This close relationship between internal and external communication has had an effect on research, where the integration of different fields has led to new concepts. In addition to strategic communication, examples of such concepts are:

- corporate communication (Cornelissen, 2011; van Riel & Fombrun, 2007)
- communication management (Nothhaft, 2010; van Ruler & Versic, 2005)
- total communication (Åberg, 1990)
- integrated internal communication (Christensen, Firat, & Cornelissen, 2009; Kalla, 2005)
- integrated communication (Lesley, 2004)
- integrated marketing communication (IMC) (Christensen, Torp, & Firat, 2005; Kliatchko, 2009)
- integrated organizational communication (Barker & Angelopulo, 2013)
- strategic integrated communication (Barker, 2013).

These relatively new concepts may be regarded as mere synonyms. The concepts have their heritage in both practitioners' and researchers' knowledge interests (see below). Researchers are usually very interested in gaining more knowledge about various phenomena, while practitioners are particularly focused on efficiency and results. For practitioners the basic idea behind the concepts is to organize the organization's communication activities in order to present a clear image of the organization to all stakeholders, and to create and maintain strong relationships with internal and external groups (Christensen, 2002; Goodman, 2000). It is fairly usual today that communication professionals make efforts to increase cooperation with marketers in order to coordinate promotional activities and thus be able to develop the organizational image, brand, and identity. As mentioned in the introductory chapter, such cooperation has been on the agenda since the mid-1980s. Equivalent cooperation is common in the field of marketing. Modern marketing theory (e.g. Grönroos, 2012; Vargo, 2011) has much in common with the thinking in public relations—that is, to identify, create, and maintain relationships with key publics. The similarity becomes even more striking when some researchers, such as Gummesson (1995), introduced the concept of relationship marketing. This perspective on marketing means a shift toward a long-term orientation in contrast to traditional marketing's short-term goal to increase sales. As discussed earlier, public relations have also moved its focus from pure information dissemination to relationship management (Cropp & Pincus, 2001). A marketing relationship is assumed to exist when the customer and the company think the same way (Grönroos, 2015). Grönroos maintains that the relationship should be mutual, meaning that the company also shows loyalty by trying to understand the needs and desires of customers, this understanding and knowledge leading to further innovation and product development and thereby more service offerings. This has certain implications for communication, which can no longer be limited to planned communication efforts but also needs to include cooperation, interaction, and dialogue. To sum up, a symmetrical relationship thinking characterizes research in strategic communication and modern research in organizational communication, public relations, and marketing communication.

Integrated marketing communication

In this section we have chosen to deal specifically with integrated marketing, which is crucial for the development of corporate communication, which in some ways is equivalent to strategic communications. Corporate communication is based in marketing and business, while strategic communication has been developed by communication researchers. We believe it is also important to understand the developments within the marketing communication field since it is a much larger field in terms of the number of professionals, researchers, and students.

Integrated marketing is a relatively new direction in the marketing field, appearing for the first time in the literature in the late 1980s (Kliatchko, 2009). A basic idea of integrated marketing is to achieve effective and efficient total communication, not only to consumers but also to other key stakeholders (Proctor & Kitchen, 2002). This is supposed to be achieved by integrating all communication activities so that a unified message reaches different target groups. The traditional view of integrated marketing is that synergy effects—when all target groups receive the same message—will lead to "one-sight, one-sound" (Kliatchko, 2009). In other words, the goal of integrated marketing is to achieve synergy and consistency in the messages to all groups (Barker, 2013; Torp, 2008).

It has long been said that we have left the solid, industrial production economy and entered a new global era with different conceptualizations; these include the information economy (first mentioned in Japan in the 1970s), the knowledge economy, the service economy, and the experience economy. In this "new economy" companies not only sell products and services but also offer such aspects as experience, community, and identity. One of the consequences of the *experience economy* is that many bookstores have undergone a metamorphosis from places of book sales to intellectual communities and scenes where customers are offered café latte, comfortable armchairs, speeches by authors, magazines, and access to the internet. Some researchers argue that the postmodern consumer no longer fits the idealized image of the rational consumer that has been dominant in marketing (Proctor & Kitchen, 2002). The new consumer is irrational, emotion-driven, and disloyal to brands and consumes in order to strengthen their self-image. This development is contrary to early criticism of marketing (Fromm, 1978), which considered it a means to undermine people's critical thinking in order to increase the sales of products that were not really needed. Contemporary critical and skeptical consumers do not accept organizations' traditional intent to persuade them with mass messages distributed through impersonal channels. These critical groups also view companies as political entities—and expect them to act as socially responsible organizations.

According to contemporary research, consumption should not be seen as a passive process in which consumers unpack and receive a given message the way the producer intended. Rather, consumption is an active and creative process in which people's identities are continually created and recreated. When a person buys something—for example, a car or clothes—she may strengthen her identity in both her own eyes and those of others. In the experience economy the boundary between producers and consumers becomes increasingly blurred (Tsai, 2005). Consumer's experiences are at the center and it is the consumers that both define and create value based on the product or service and the values that the organization has put into the brand.

There are many explanations for the emergence of integrated marketing communication. One explanation is that markets are becoming harder and harder to predict, access, and control. Classic marketing theory and practice demands that marketers should assess and adjust the organization's offer to customers' needs and expectations. However, this becomes increasingly difficult as customer preferences become unclear and constantly change due to more travel and easy access to mass and social media that provide a flow of new impulses and ideas. Integrated marketing can hence be understood as a tool to control and manage today's complex markets (Christensen et al., 2005).

Another explanation can be traced to the poor self-image of the public relations industry. Those dealing with public relations, both practitioners and academics, have good reason to bring to the fore the new concept of integrated marketing and make inroads into marketers' traditional domains. In the early 1990s, several US university communication programs experienced problems due to fewer qualified applicants (while the number of applicants for business schools increased). Further, fewer communication students got qualified jobs, but the number of master's theses in public relations continued to grow (Spotts, Lambert, & Joyce, 1998). At the same time, public relations departments at US universities had rather few teachers with a doctorate (Ph.D.) and consequently had lower status among colleagues in the communication departments. As a solution to these problems teachers began to sketch out and develop integrated bachelor programs in public relations, marketing, and advertising. The basic idea was that students that were enrolled in the new educational programs would have a better chance to work across departmental boundaries. Integrated marketing can accordingly be perceived as a tool that academics in public relations can use to take shares from and exploit the power and attraction of the marketing field.

Public relations and marketing researchers and integrated marketing communication

Researchers in public relations often stress that the field is a critical element of integrated marketing communications, while public relations as such has a long-term perspective. What drives public relations is the desire to create strong relationships and strong brands rather than just increase short-term sales and profits. Furthermore, public relations researchers believe that they take a broader approach, not only focusing on customers but also establishing good relationships with stakeholders such as employees, citizens, politicians, investors, suppliers, dealers, and journalists. These stakeholders are considered more important for the development of the organization's brand and image in the long run—yes, more important because employees, investors, and governmental authorities can affect the organization even more severely than customers (Moriarty, 1997).

A clear majority of public relations researchers respond positively to the concept of integrated marketing, but there are also some critics. Researchers such as Cropp and Pincus (2001) and Hutton (2001) warn of a "marketing-imperialism", which implies that marketers take over the activities of communication professionals and, by extension, lower their status and independence and render them obsolete.

However, some researchers in the field of marketing are also critical of integrated marketing as a concept. They see it as "the emperor's new clothes" and say there is nothing new under the sun, even though proponents of developed integrated marketing present it as a radically new idea. Proponents claim that traditional marketing is dead and that the conventional marketing mix (the four Ps—product, price, place, and promotion), which is seen as the marketer's toolbox (Ellis et al., 2011), is no longer valid. As an alternative to the traditional product-oriented marketing mix, Schultz, Tannenbaum, and Lauterborn (1993) launched the four Cs (consumer, consumer cost, convenience, and communication), which is a more customer-oriented model. Furthermore, proponents underline the importance of relationship marketing and customer communications and thus reject traditional marketing that has a one-sided sales focus. Critics argue that integrated marketing communication has systematically ignored sixty years of marketing literature. For example, already in the 1930s researchers noted the need for integration of the various parts of the promotion (e.g. advertising, public relations, and personal selling). According to the critics, integrated marketing has produced a complete confusion of boundaries, confusing terminology and a revision of concepts, which in turn negatively affects the thinking and understanding. The only people who have something to gain from this trend are communication researchers (Spotts et al., 1998). Marketing researchers (e.g. Barker, 2013) have also questioned the value of integrated marketing, since research demonstrating its effectiveness and impact is mostly anecdotal. It should be emphasized that it is difficult to empirically demonstrate these forms of communication effects since they are usually indirect and long term.

Pros and cons of integrated communication

It is possible to identify both clear advantages and clear disadvantages of the "integrated trend" in the academic literature. We will now present some of these advantages and disadvantages.

If we start with the disadvantages, it is obvious that the integrated trend has arisen out of a desire to better, faster, and more effectively reach out to different publics with the same message. The goal of integrated communication is to demonstrate a clear and unambiguous image of what an organization stands for in all messages, symbols, and strategies. The overall goal is having control of a world that has become increasingly difficult to understand and predict. Integrated communication is here perceived as an effective tool to capture and restrain the new and constantly changing world that some authors call the postmodern world (e.g. Proctor & Kitchen, 2002). This should be conducted through an integration of all media and messages, which avoids inconsistency. Since humans think and act according to their beliefs, the idea is that a strong brand (which is the perception of an organization) should be the foundation of a successful organization. The idea is that a strong brand can help people choose between different alternatives and make them have a positive view of the organization. A risk with the integrated communications trend is that we get stuck in a traditional and simplistic understanding of recipients. It is assumed that receivers will be affected by an organizational message if all messages are consistent. What is put at the center is the formulation and distribution of messages.

A fundamental problem is that organizations have never been able to control how recipients perceive and interpret a message, not even in the childhood of commercialism. In their book *Brand Anarchy* (2012), Earl and Waddington emphasize that the ability of organizations to control a message has deteriorated considerably with digital communication and the internet. In line with the product mix model—the four Cs (see above)—it will be even more important to develop the integrated marketing communications to develop greater customer engagement and thus involvement (Kliatchko, 2009). An ideal that is promoted within marketing communication nowadays is co-creation— terms such as *co*-production, *co*-management, and *co*llaborative management have therefore appeared. Social media have changed the conditions for organizations to work with communication and relationship building with different stakeholders. Even if recipients have never been passive or non-reflexive, the opportunities to check, create, influence, recreate, and criticize organizations' messages have never been as good as they are today. In addition, recipients communicate and discuss with other consumers via blogs, Twitter, Facebook, etc., and thus reach out to a large number of people. Even if the internet has been around since 1995, the spread and development of technology facilitated communication between consumers and thus increased the power of consumers in relation to organizations. It is therefore possible to speak of a paradigm shift in strategic communication, which means that thinking is no longer based on theories of mass media research. An obvious consequence of this is that the work and thinking of communication professionals must change and adapt to a new situation. This process has started, but it will take a long time to mature while the traditional approach is so entrenched (Falkheimer & Heide, 2014).

Integrated marketing communication is too narrow a concept and wrongly signals that communication is simply all about marketing. It may be that integrated marketing can work in a business context, but in terms of other organizations, such as municipalities, hospitals, or government agencies, the concept in general is not useful. Over the last decades we have witnessed how, as a result of new public management, marketing concepts have been used even within governmental organizations, defining patients, pupils, and students as customers. Marketing terminology leads these thoughts, and maybe even the documents, in a wrong direction.

We believe that it is easy to be blinded by the light, too driven by a desire to integrate messages and media, and as a result forget how complex the human interpretation process is and how different we are as people. We all have different interests, experiences, and knowledge and we are all part of different networks and interpret information based on this. It is obviously important that an organization's messages do not run counter to each other (for example, that a newspaper does not announce that organization X will terminate two hundred people in manufacturing when on the same day the business section reports unusually good financial developments). However, it is not possible to face up to and manage a complex environment using simple models and processes (Weick, 1995). Integrated communications can be seen as an attempt to control the ambiguous and rapidly changing environment by means of more uniformity. But in practice it is highly questionable whether an organization could ever control communications in all forms and at all levels.

A clear example of a "failed" attempt to achieve integrated communication is the trend to make organizations transparent, both internally and externally. Organizations are now under pressure—for example, through legislation (annual and environmental reports) and through the media that scrutinizes organizations—to present as much information as possible to different stakeholders. Information and communication technology also enables organizations to easily and rapidly publish information. This means that organizations can be perceived as more transparent than before, but also more vulnerable. The situation is somewhat ironic. First, there is in the literature an implicit notion that outside groups want or require organizations to be transparent. Second, communication is believed to be the same as information, and it is assumed that publics want more and more information. Third, it is assumed that more information helps publics develop a more sophisticated understanding of an organization (Christensen, 2002). Research has shown that most consumers, other than specific professional or interest groups, are not interested or involved in what the organizations wish to say (Christensen & Cheney, 2000). Another factor is that even if external teams were interested and had access to all possible information, humans lack the capacity to deal with such volume (Christensen, 2002). Already in 1956 the Nobel laureate in economics Herbert Simon emphasized that human beings have limited rationality—that is, we are not able to process all information and must content ourselves with a satisfactory result. In addition, an imperfect ability to process information often requires adequate knowledge and interpretation frames for it to be understood. For example, you do not understand much of a balance sheet or an income statement without basic knowledge of economics. Consequently, an organization cannot be sure how a person interprets information. In other words, it seems like *mission impossible* to reach a general and agreed understanding of an organizational image.

A clear advantage of integrated communications is that they can help raise the status and increase awareness of communication issues and communication aspects of organizational processes such as organizational change and organizational learning. With a strong communications department it is easier to build up extensive expertise in the field and provide more opportunities to work on strategically optimal communication issues where the boundary between internal and external communication is erased. It should also be noted that the integrated led to a new focus on overall consistency in brand communication in relation to the organization's overall strategies, not—as before—only on tactics such as message and media integration. This has allowed researchers—for example, Barker (2013)—to suggest that it is appropriate to use the term strategic integrated communications.

In conclusion, two parallel developments have taken place within the field of marketing and the field of communication. Integrated marketing was developed in the field of marketing and strategic communications grew within the field of communication. In both fields the researchers identified the need to take a holistic approach to organizations' communication because the boundary between internal and external communication is artificial. Organizations' communications must be linked and related to the organization's operations and overall goals and strategies.

Strategic communication as a knowledge and research field

If you look through publications within the field of strategic communication, it becomes obvious that it there is a jungle of flourishing concepts that are used as synonyms for each other. In different texts you find public relations, communication management, and organizational communication used interchangeably. Among practitioners it is a common understanding that strategic communication includes the management of all communication functions in an organization, whereas public relations is perceived as a special function along with investor relations, marketing, and internal communications. While there are those who see public relations as an overall strategic concept, others perceive it as different communication techniques to produce pseudo-events (i.e. planned to give an organization publicity), press releases, and websites. In academia, strategic communication is a knowledge interest that we find among researchers in fields such as business administration, sociology, psychology, political science, and media and communication studies. This interest is all about communication and organizations that understand the organizational processes from a communicative perspective. It is foremost researchers in the research fields of marketing, public relations, and organizational communication that have focused on strategic communication. Unfortunately, researchers in these three fields have worked rather isolated from each other, with no major exchange of experience or knowledge. This tendency is common in academia and researchers are often inclined to isolate themselves and fight their own corner, but it is especially true of new fields where there is a need to draw a clear line to the "parent" subject. While this is understandable and probably strategically wise, it does not benefit the development of the knowledge interest. There is also a risk that the wheel is constantly reinvented, with isolated researchers working on research questions that are already answered or duplicating models and theories. This isolation tendency has meant, among other things, that joint projects have been few and researchers have published their results in subject-specific magazines (more on this below). This tendency is obviously problematic and there is always a danger that the research becomes disparate and incomplete.

The problem with the traditional understanding of strategic communication is that it explicitly focuses on communication per se and the various activities linked to it. In an analogy with Stanley Deetz' definition of organizational communication, we would like to suggest that strategic communication can be seen, perhaps even primarily, as actors applying a communicative perspective to organizational processes: trying to understand and explain, for example, organizational change, leadership, quality, cooperation, and learning in relation to communication theories and all aspects of communication.

Strategic communication as a research field is the study of organizations' communication (Verhoeven, Zerfass, & Tench, 2011). We therefore need to take a holistic approach to communication, which involves studying organizations' communication at various levels: individual, group, organizational, and societal. Thus, strategic communication is a knowledge field that includes both formal and informal communication. A knowledge interest is linked to research, the development of theories, and methods to reflect, criticize, and develop the practice. An interest in strategic communication can be found in many disciplines, but it is above all communication researchers who put communication at the center and also adopt a communicative perspective on organizational processes and thereby develop some understanding and knowledge of the "reality". Within the research fields of public relations and organizational communication, communication and communications issues used to be the focus of researchers' interest. Today, however, more and more researchers adopt a communicative perspective on organizations and their activities (Deetz, 2001; Verčič, van Ruler, & Flodin, 2001).

A comparison of strategic communication and its cousin corporate communication (see above) reveals a crucial difference. Within the field of strategic communication, most researchers have abandoned the early communication models and instead take the ritual view of communication (see Chapter 1) (Falkheimer & Heide, 2014). This means that communication is perceived as the very mean that creates and provides the conditions for an organization's existence. This is closely related to the social constructionist perspective of science philosophy, where organizations are not considered as fixed objects but rather as continuous construction processes. An English business administration academic, Robert Chia (1995), used the term *becoming* to describe this approach to organizations, which should be compared to the opposite understanding, in which organizations are regarded as solid and stable objects. A researcher who pointed out the fundamental relationship between communication and organization early on is the American social psychologist Karl E. Weick, who we mentioned in the introductory chapter. Weick (1995) argued that the concept *organizing* is better than organization, which indicates something stable and unchanging. According to Weick, communication can even be understood as a synonym of organizing, it being impossible to imagine an organization without communication.

However, researchers in corporate communication tend to start from a transmission view of communication, where communication is seen rather as a tool through which various desirable effects can be achieved (Christensen & Cornelissen, 2011). A dominating management perspective is also significant for corporate communication research—here, researchers are primarily interested in studying how organizations can become more efficient in order to strengthen organizational competitiveness.

Many researchers in strategic communication have a rather traditional management perspective, but there are some whose primary interest is increasing our understanding of organizations' communication. For example, Derina Holtzhausen (2012) underlines that too many communication researchers do not see "dialogue" as a key element of "strategic". These researchers understand strategic communication as one-way manipulation and persuasion and it is therefore inevitable that they only take a management perspective. The problem, though, is that this fails to highlight the complexity of organizations' communication. For example, there are many ways to understand an organization's rationality. Employees frequently perceive the organization and its communication differently from the management. Thus, one way to get away from the traditional management perspective in strategic communication is to study phenomena from an employee perspective. So far only a few studies have adopted this perspective (e.g. Falkheimer et al., 2017; Heide & Simonsson, 2011). By studying strategic communication from several different perspectives it is possible to get a more holistic and equitable view (Hallahan et al., 2007). The ideal of a holistic image of strategic communication may also be achieved by gaining inspiration from other disciplines, such as communication and media, and from sociological, organizational and management theory (see Figure 3.1).

Strategic communication as a practice

Strategic communication is not limited to the activities of communication professionals. Zerfass and Huck (2007, p. 108) argue that strategic communication as a practice "shapes meaning, builds trust, creates reputation, and manages symbolic relationships with internal and external stakeholders in order to support organizational growth and secure the freedom to operate." It is also very much about the work done by marketers, HR staff, quality control staff, and managers at different hierarchical levels, and it is also all about the contacts that employees—that is, representatives of the organization—have with different stakeholders. An organization's communication creates, maintains, adjusts, and consolidates the perception and image of the organization, its activities and fundamental values. Communication is, as noted several times, the foundation of organizational existence (Putnam & Nicotera, 2010). This does not mean that an understanding of the importance of communication is found among all organizational members or that everyone has the same education in communication. The communication professionals are still the communication experts in an organization and should be used in this role as internal consultants (Heide & Simonsson, 2011, 2014)

The practical work of strategic communication is often called communication management. This encompasses management's communication with employees through formal communication channels that follow the organizational structure. Examples of formal communication are information provided by the HR manager at a major meeting and emails from the CEO about a forthcoming organizational change. Formal communication also includes employee communications and feedback to the manager and employee in formal contexts. Informal communication is the other form of communication—usually it is interpersonal, but it also includes gossip and rumors.

Strategic communication can be described as a fundamental part of an organization's management function and a practical field of specialization that includes the exploration of needs, planning, strategic formulation,

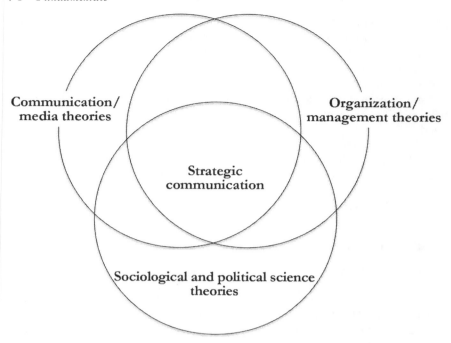

Figure 3.1 Relationship to other disciplines
Source: Falkheimer and Heide (2014).

communication interventions, communication programs, and communication processes. As a practice, strategic communication includes communication that helps the organization to reach set goals. Being strategic is about doing the right things—that is, contributing to the organization's success and long-term survival (Zerfass & Huck, 2007). Strategic communication includes all forms of communication—internal and external, formal and informal—that are consistent with overall values and visions of the organization. Strategic communication occurs at all levels of an organization—for example, in a manager's daily communication with his employees, in a staff editor's or web editor's work, and in a marketing director's or communication director's work on communication policy and communication strategy.

Research on communication professionals

One of the most researched fields in public relations is the roles, duties, and functions of professional communicators (e.g. Grunig, Grunig, & Dozier, 2006; Grunig, Grunig, & Dozier, 2002). The focus of this research has been describing the different roles and such aspects as gender, power, and influence in the organization's strategic decision-making. Roles are about the expectations of organizational members—that is, how they are expected to act in different situations (Fondas & Stewart, 1994; Tindall & Holtzhausen, 2011). Organization members' tasks and responsibilities are thus divided into different roles. Research on professional communicators has often led to different role typologies—systematic classifications of types that have common characteristics. Amongst the first researchers who produced a role typology of professional communicators were Broom and Smith (1979). Their typology consists of four different roles:

- the decision maker
- the communication facilitator
- the problem solver
- the communications technician.

However, Broom and Smith's typology is not based on any empirical research but is purely theoretical and normative. Thus, Broom and Smith wished to explain how it *should* be and how professional communicators *should* work. This could be understood from the view of communication professionals of that time—when they primarily were understood as responsible for information distribution (Bell & Bell, 1976). Later research has shown that the first three roles are closely related, which has reduced the roles to two, the so-called strategist–technician dichotomy (Dozier, 1992; Dozier & Broom, 1995). An important conclusion of James Grunig with colleagues' (2002) excellency theory is that excellent communication departments have the ability and knowledge to carry out a strategic role. Other researchers (e.g. Creedon, 1991; Toth, Serini, Wright, & Emig, 1998) emphasize that the technician–strategist dichotomy is too simple and categorical. Moss, Newman, and DeSanto (2005) stress that the view of the management function has been considered too unilaterally. Instead, researchers should between management tasks/responsibilities and behaviors.

What is missing, therefore, are the important questions how and why, which can be answered primarily through qualitative studies (i.e. interviews and observations rather than questionnaires). When we meet practitioners in different contexts, they often emphasize that the technical and strategic roles are closely interrelated and cannot be separated. For example, the communications manager must also have knowledge of how to perform technical tasks such as writing press releases or updating a web page. This view is reinforced by recent role research (e.g. Tindall & Holtzhausen, 2011; Werder & Holtzhausen, 2011): the strategic role is closely linked to all communication roles. However, Cornelissen (2011) writes that one problem is that many practitioners have little desire to take on a strategic role and prefer to confine their careers to technical specialization and skills. They simply feel more secure in this role and are wary of stepping outside it. This means that communication professionals are particularly happy when they get a new medium they can commit to. Two examples of such new media might be intranets and social media. Another problem with this focus on new media is it encourages practitioners to abandon a more complex view of communication and fall back on the transmission view of communication, a tendency that is often totally unreflected.

Research on communication professionals has also highlighted their role as actors of cross boundaries—for example, as mediators between management and employees, management and journalists, and management and environmental activists (e.g. Kim & Reber, 2009; Steyn & Niemann, 2010). The task of communication professionals is thus to understand and present the "others'" perspective to the leadership so that management can make the best possible decisions. Van Riel (1995) calls this assignment the mirror function, which in practice involves issues management—scanning changes and trends in the environment and predicting how these can affect the organization, as well as being prepared for various forms of communication effort. The mirror function includes mapping key stakeholders (those who have an interest in the organization and who may in some way affect or be affected by the organization's activities), gather press clippings, follow the debate in relevant subjects, and recognize changes in the internal communication environment. Dozier, Grunig, and Grunig (1995) also see worldwide issues management as a key way for communication professionals to gain access to the management team. In addition to the importance of cross boundaries, the relational aspect has been highlighted by several researchers (Choi & Choi, 2009; Gregory, 2008). This means that communication professionals should have a high level of skill in creating and maintaining good relationships with key stakeholders and thus the ability to network and represent the organization.

An important prerequisite for communication professionals to be able to act as professionals is that they have access to management or to what is often called the dominant coalition (Grunig et al., 2002). This term was coined by the organizational researchers Cyert and March (1963) to refer to the social network within an organization that has the greatest influence on the goals that are chosen and the design of strategies. The dominant coalition consists of not only members of the management group (the formal group) but also those within a more informal group. Members of this informal group might include, for example, persons with large networks or expert knowledge. Research has shown that there are five main ways to gain access to the dominant coalition (Bowen, 2009):

- organization crisis
- ethical dilemmas
- credibility issues that have arisen over time
- issues that are high on the media agenda
- leadership.

Of these five ways, the organizational crisis is the most important route to accessing the dominant coalition (cf. Falkheimer & Heide, 2010). Communication professionals who have proficient knowledge in and experience of crisis communication thus have the best qualifications for achieving a high level of legitimacy in an organization. Another important prerequisite is that the communicator has advanced knowledge in leadership and organizational leadership (Kinnick & Cameron, 1994). In recent research on communication professionals (e.g. Steyn, 2009), it is stated that communication professionals who wish to develop their career and move up the organization hierarchy must master the role of educator and strategist (and reflexive thinker). This has previously been emphasized by researchers (e.g. Verčič et al., 2001), who claim that the reflexive characteristic is typical of European communication professionals. Other researchers (Heide & Simonsson, 2011; Zerfass & Franke, 2013) emphasize that it is the role of the internal consultant to develop an organization into a communicative organization and thus strengthen the role of communication professionals in the organization. The internal consultant will serve as an important resource educating employees and managers in communication—for example, helping make meetings more effective and improving the management's talks with staff. If the role of the internal communication consultant is to succeed, communication must be linked to business strategies so that it can support and promote work towards achieving the goals (Verhoeven et al., 2011). According to Verhoeven and colleagues, there are at least two ways in which the communication aspect can be linked to business strategies. First, communication professionals can help find communication solutions to problems arising from business strategies, such as developing sales through better communication with consumers or enhancing motivation and commitment among employees through a more open communication environment. Second, communicator professionals can contribute by making evident the communication aspects of different strategic decisions, such as reflecting on possible effects on the organization's reputation or on employees' long-term commitment and pride in being employees of the organization.

Communicators should be professional, but this does not mean that the profession itself is a profession—rather, it is a so-called semi-profession. There are various different definitions of a profession and communication professionals meet some of the criteria that are commonly mentioned: there is qualified higher education related to the profession, specific tasks, and a professional code. However, the professional roles are quite different in different countries and cultures, and the ethical code that exists (often produced by a national profession association) does not have the anchorage or sanction system associated with, for example, doctors and lawyers. Although many communication professionals in most countries have a higher education in the field of communication, there are diverse backgrounds (Falkheimer & Heide, 2014), these courses differ a lot.

Responsibilities of communication professionals

- Design the organization's communication structure, i.e. select which media to use and in what situations.

- Define communication principles and standards.
- Formulate communication goals.
- Manage and evaluate the flow of information.
- Design crisis communication.
- Design and implement communication strategies.
- Constitute the eyes and ears of the management, i.e. monitor the outside world and the organization and report on various changes.
- Act as an internal consultant on communication issues and train staff in communication.

Research shows that European communication managers, unlike those in the US, are increasingly working as educators—that is, teaching other members of the organization in order to increase managers' and coworkers' communication skills (Verhoeven et al., 2011). It is also argued that European communication professionals are more reflexive than their US colleagues (van Ruler & Verčič, 2004). Reflexivity means here that communication professionals try to take an outward perspective (the perspective of external stakeholders such as shareholders, citizens, and politicians) in order to better predict and understand stakeholders' perceptions and actions. In Europe, organizations' social legitimacy is emphasized more than in the North American context. Consequently, trust issues become fundamental to European communication professionals.

Research journals within the field

There are specific research journals for each of the three fields, public relations, organizational communication, and marketing communication. Of these three, marketing is the most major in terms of both the amount of research and the number of students. It is therefore to be expected that the marketing field has the most research journals. Over the last decades, new journals have been established that are based on a more holistic approach to organization's communication. The different types of communication that occur within an organization are intimately linked and the traditional division of internal and external communication is both unnatural and artificial. This insight has led to a new direction in the field of strategic communication, which may be traced back to the early 1990s. More and more marketing researchers in those years began to focus on relations and branding, and researchers in organizational communication also began to study the relationship between internal and external communication. And in public relations, scholars became increasingly interested in internal communication and its connection to external communication activities. These developments prompted the launch of several new scientific journals. *Corporate Communications: An International Journal* was launched in 1996, covering both external communication (related to reputation, image, and crisis communication) and internal communication (such as leadership communication and change communication). The *Journal of Communication Management*, first published in 1996, also takes a broad approach to the field of strategic communication but specifically seeks to share knowledge between those who study communication management and those who practice it by publishing theoretical and empirical research. The latest addition is the *International Journal of Strategic Communication*, launched in 2006. Its purpose is to cover "multidisciplinary" research on the role of communication from an organizational management perspective.

Research journals in strategic communication and related fields

Strategic communication

Business Communication Quarterly
Corporate Communications: An international Journal
International Journal of Strategic Communication
Journal of Applied Communication Research
Journal of Communication Management
Journal of Communication Inquiry

Marketing and marketing communication

International Journal of Integrated Marketing Communications
Journal of Marketing
Journal of Marketing Communications
Journal of the Academy of Marketing Science
Marketing Theory
European Journal of Marketing

Organizational communication

Journal of Business Communication
Management Communication Quarterly

Public relations

Journal of Public Relations Research
Public Relations Inquiry
Public Relations Review
Public Relations Quarterly

Organization and management studies

Academy of Management Journal
Academy of Management Review

Human Relations
Journal of Management
Journal of Management Studies
Organization
Organization Science
Organization Studies
International Journal of Organizational Analysis
Scandinavian Journal of Management
Sloan Management Review
The Academy of Management Annals

A selection of associations for communication professionals

- Arthur W. Page Society—a professional association for senior corporate communications executives, aiming to strengthen the profession. See www.awpagesociety.com.
- EUPRERA—the European Public Relations Education and Research Association has 500 members from 40 countries that are interested in advancing academic research and knowledge in strategic communication. See www.euprera.eu.
- CIPR—the Chartered Institute of Public Relations is the association for public relations professionals in Great Britain and the largest professional body outside North America. See www.cipr.co.uk.
- COMMUNICATION DIRECTOR—is a quarterly magazine for in-house corporate communications and public relations in Europe. Communication Director is partner with the European Association of Communication Directors (EACD). See www.communication-director.com.
- Global Alliance for Public Relations and Communication Management— a confederation of the world's major PR and communication management associations and institutions, representing 160,000 professional and academic members. See www.globalalliancepr.org.
- IABC—the International Association of Business Communicators is a professional network formed in 1970, with about 15,000 members from more than eighty countries. The purpose of IABC is to increase members' knowledge, networking, and delivery of vacancies. See www.iabc.com.
- ICA—the International Communication Association is an academic association for practitioners and researchers that are interested in the various aspects of communication. ICA is a non-governmental association recognized by the United Nations. See www.icahdq.org.
- IPRA—the International Public Relations Association represents individual public relations professionals around the world. IPRA hosts international public relations conferences and events. See www.ipra.org.

- Melcrum is a network focusing on internal communication and spreading best practices to its members. Melcrum also conducts its own research and the results are presented on the website. See www.melcrum.com.
- PRWeek is one of the largest trade magazines of the field of public relations and aimed primarily at professional communicators. See www.prweek.com.
- PRSA—the Public Relations Society of America is an US association for public relations professionals that also encompasses the Public Relations Student Society of America. See www.prsa.org.
- Social Media Association—the association helps communication professionals to map and follow the development of social media and its use by organizations with events and a blog. See www.socialmediaassoc.com.

On becoming a reflexive practitioner

Today it appears that there is a rather large distance between strategic communication as a practice and strategic communication as a research field. While the research has come relatively far, practice seems to be stuck in the same place as before. Grunig, Grunig, and Dozier (2006), along with their co-authors, noted that "public relations practitioners continue to think of public relations as mostly publicity and media relations." The weakness of some communication professionals is that they have excellent subject-specific knowledge but major knowledge gaps in other topics relevant to an organization. Examples of such subjects are business administration, political science, commercial law, and marketing. Without these subject skills it is difficult to take a more comprehensive and strategic approach to the organization's communication issues, and the risk is that communicators can only deal with technical issues. At the same time, it must be acknowledged that more and more modern communication professionals have had a broad-based education, so the future looks brighter for this group and their role and function in organizations. However, a major challenge for many communication professionals is that they are caught up in an endless chain of expectations and deliveries (see Figure 3.2). Leaders and management in organizations have various expectations of communication professionals and what they should and could deliver. These expectations will influence what communication professionals prioritize amongst all possible tasks and strategies. There is of course a strong relation between managers' expectations of the communication department and how it is assessed and valued. Since communications are often indirect and long term in their effects, it is difficult to evaluate and measure. Consequently, when communication and the communication department are evaluated the focus is often on tangibles such as press clippings, channels, articles, and different forms of text production. In other words, the evaluations mainly focus on the *means* of communication

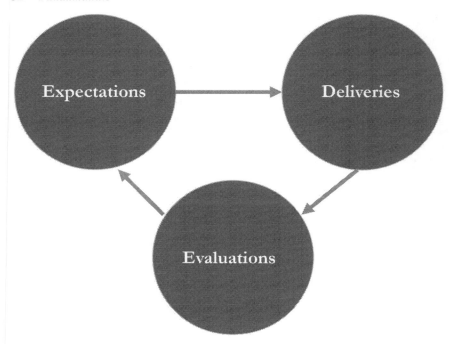

Figure 3.2 The chain of expectations, evaluation, and deliveries

rather the *effects*, these being more difficult to measure. Ergo, organizational managers often expect communication professionals to deliver different forms of media content and to manage organizational media such as the intranet, web pages, social media, and staff magazines. It is therefore understandable that many communication professionals deliver what is expected of them and what is evaluated. As organizational consultants we often meet practitioners who struggle with communication challenges that are based on the management team's idea of what needs to be done communicatively. For example, the management may have an idea that all organizational members in a large organization with many sub-brands should suddenly identify with the overall owner-brand. The practitioner may ask us: "What shall we do to reach this goal—shall we use storytelling and social media or some other channel?" Other practitioners struggle with being required to engage all organizational members in the organization strategy. In the article "Doing the right things or doing things right", we and our co-authors (Falkheimer et al., 2016) discuss the challenges that modern communication professionals confront. They can focus either on *doing things right*—that is, more or less being "their master's voice" and acting as a megaphone calling out different messages—or on *doing the right things*—that is, acting strategically. In practice, no such dichotomy exists: the modern communication practitioner must have knowledge and skills in both technical and strategic aspects of strategic communication. We underline in the article that communication professionals who do not master the technical side of the profession risk being seen as fluffy strategists.

The above examples of challenges that many communication professionals face can be put in the "doing things right" category. What we find rather striking is that communication professionals try to solve tasks they have been given by management even if their professional knowledge and training tells them that these tasks are more or less impossible. To do things right is rather simple, since it a matter of performing and solving technical tasks. Acting strategically is more complex and challenging. We argue that working strategically is all too often related to one-dimensional rationalistic ideas of management. This includes the idea that managers can control and steer organizations, communication, and the surrounding environment—that is, a management logic. It is also related to an idea that it is easy to measure return on investment when it comes to communication. Managerialism can be contrasted to communication professionalism, which values things other than direct return on investment. The challenge is that strategic communication is a soft power discipline and communication professionals must develop alternative arguments and show communication impacts that convince management of its value. This is closely related to communication professionalism, which arises when communication professionals work according to the principles of strategic communication. This includes being communication advocates and seeing and analyzing important organizational decisions from a communication perspective. Hence, communication professionals need to argue for the value of strategic communication as engaged coworkers who act as organizational ambassadors and maintain and improve the reputation of the organization.

Part II

Communication processes and organizations

4 Society, social change and strategic communication

In the introductory chapter of this section, the aim is to describe and analyze strategic communication in society. As already indicated, one can view and understand strategic communication via two different approaches: one organizational and the other societal. Ideally, professionals develop a double competence and are able to see the bigger picture and avoid getting stuck in an organization-centric view. The ability to see an organization from an external point of view is crucial for adding value to organizations. There are several possible constructs for this external analysis, especially regarding the public element. In public relations theory, *publics* are in focus (Grunig, 1997), defined from an organizational perspective. Situational publics are described in the chapter about communication and defined as spontaneous formations of people constructed in relation to a problem or dispute that exists or is created between an organization and its surroundings. In business administration and corporate communication, the concept publics is replaced with *stakeholders.* This concept has its origin in the strategic management work of the economist R. Edward Freeman (1984). Stakeholders are different actors that can or may be affected by an organization, and interact and communicate with the organization. They are viewed as more active actors than *publics* and less anonymous. Stakeholders are directly or indirectly influenced by and may influence the operations of organizations. A third construct that has been widely used, especially in campaign planning and market communications, is *target group.* A target group is a group of individuals, usually segmented by demographic variables, that an organization wants to reach and persuade. The concept is linked to the transmission communication perspective and implies that these groups are passive receivers of a message, at most steered by psychological mechanisms, in a mass communication process. Fourth, one may use the concept *public opinion,* put forward by the reporter and political analyst Walter Lippmann (1922/1997) in his classic book *Public Opinion.* Public opinion is a debated concept but may be described as the collective preferences of a mass of people (usually in a national context) in relation to government and politics. Finally, we may use the concept of *public sphere,* as discussed earlier with reference to Jürgen Habermas, to help understand public discussion in a society. From a strategic communication angle all concepts are possible, but the concept stakeholder may be of particular value since it implies a concrete and active view of the external actors of relevance for organizational goal-oriented communications.

Strategic communication as a professional field is dependent on social change. One may even view strategic communication as a consequence of the social change that has been analyzed for decades by social theorists: from modernity to late modernity. According to this interpretation, strategic communication is mirroring the structural changes that in turn may be explained as driven by technological, political, economic, and cultural factors. Public relations, marketing communication, and organizational communication are disciplines developed during modernity in the last centuries, while strategic communication is a transboundary and late modern field of knowledge.

> It is important to note that these disciplines were developed as specialty functions in the modernistic world of the 20th century. Yet, at the beginning of the twenty-first century, these disciplines function in a postmodern environment that stresses a more holistic approach to examining organizational phenomena, while having to deal with increasingly fragmented audiences and delivery platforms.
>
> (Hallahan et al., 2007, p. 4)

Below we explain what social theorists means with modernity and late modernity, aiming to increase the understanding of our field from a historical and societal perspective.

Modernity: Rationalism, objectivity and individualism

Modernity is the scientific movement and societal paradigm founded during the Enlightenment of the late seventeenth century in the Western world. Modernity is defined by rationalism, objectivity, and individualism. Rationalism means basing opinions and actions on reason (logical thinking or empirical investigations) rather than emotions or traditions. Objectivity means that we distance ourselves from our emotions and subjective ideas and try to isolate facts from personal views. Individualism is a perception that gives individual freedom and independence the highest value.

Religion and tradition cannot be totally excluded from modernity and have in some contexts been integrated with modern thought, but they are more often transmitted from the public sphere to the private sphere. Modernity is also strongly associated with the growth of industrialism, capitalism, and the establishment of nation states. According to Thompson (1995), the development of modernity is dependent on two major social transformations. First, an economic transition from feudalism and agriculture to free trade, commerce, and industrial production systems. Second, the political transition from small states or regions to nation states with professional bureaucracies and military systems. The nation state is typical of modernity and has been a framework for cultural identities for a couple of hundred years. It is different from nationalism, which has the same time frame but is based on romanticism and the idea that some nations are better than others.

Mass media, from the daily press to radio and television, has been of vital importance for the modern transition in society. Journalism, advertising, and public relations are strongly connected to the establishment of mass communication systems as well as to the nation states, governmental bureaucracies, and the growth of corporations. Communication functions, such as marketing and communication departments, follow the logic of modern administration and organizational management (e.g. the division of labor). The divisions between specialized units and the distinction between external and internal communication is also modern in this sense. In modernity, communication functions are supposed to increase organizational efficiency by adapting to traditional strategic ideas of planning and standardization. Scientific empirical methods (e.g. the asymmetrical two-step model) are used to make rational decisions.

Late modernity

For several years, social theorists have used different concepts and explanations to describe the transition from modernity to something else. French philosophers (e.g. Lyotard, 1996) were already declaring in the 1980s that modernity was being replaced by a new social order: postmodernity, defined as opposite to modern society and modernist traits. Postmodern theories oppose the idea of universal theories that explain the world. The modernistic belief in science and rational thought is challenged and the grand narratives (explaining history, science, human progress, etc.) are deconstructed. Postmodernists do not use causal explanations (x gives y) to explain the world, but focus on the role of language (e.g. discourses and narratives) and subjectivity. But postmodernity, as mentioned earlier, is a multifaceted concept, and used in different ways. It is both a philosophy of ideas and a theoretical framework that tries to explain the current social order. From a social theoretical perspective, postmodernity is connected to structural trends such as globalization (financial, cultural, political), diversity (migration and polarization), consumerism (late capitalism), mediatization (where mediated communication saturates relationships and processes), activism (challenging authorities) and post-Fordism (organizational networks and new modes of organizing labor). In the postmodern world there is no longer any link between the really existing world and the symbols that represent it; instead we find ourselves in a hyper-reality where the characters communicate with each other and create an imaginary reality, according to another main proponent (Baudrillard, 1994).

Several social theorists opposed the ideas of postmodernity and the idea that postmodern society is radically new. Instead, these social theorists define contemporary society as late modern, reflexive, or liquid modernity, seeing the new social order as in fact a deepening of modernity. One of these theorists is

Anthony Giddens (1990), who distinguished core processes of change in society from modernity to late modernity: the expansive spread of modern institutions at the global level and increased pace of change. Giddens has described three characteristics of late modernity. First, Giddens points to the *separation (or compression) of space and time*, how media facilitates communication between people. Second, he points to the *disembedding of social systems*, how social relations are lifted out of local space (e.g. through expert systems such as computerized networks) and opened up for new social formations. Finally, he highlights reflexivity, *the reflexive appropriation of knowledge*, the process by which we humans constantly reflect on our actions and our position, a process that is extended through the production of more and more information and knowledge about our social life.

The sociologist Zygmunt Bauman (2000) differentiates between solid society and liquid society, the former being characterized by the centralization of diverse institutions and by clear roles for different actors in society. In this societal structure, governmental authorities, citizens, and customers have recognizable boundaries between them. Mass communication constitutes the dominant form of communication, and people define themselves through distinguishable groups. Liquid society is defined by increasing insecurity and more individual choice. Individuals experience increased uncertainty and continually re-examine their relationships in accordance with how they interpret new information. The transparent boundaries that define "solid" society are constantly challenged. In a liquid society, everyone is a sender or a participant.

Media researcher James Lull (2007) focuses on media trends. Lull means that we now live in a world where two conflicting media cultures collide: cultures based on different models of communication. First, we have traditional "push" media cultures, where centralized authorities and institutions deliver professional media content through controlled one-to-many channels. Audiences are seen as target groups, defined through demographic variables. Journalists and professional communicators are the senders, while citizens and customers are the recipients. He contrasts the "push" culture with the "pull" culture, which is defined as a culture where the needs and interests of groups or individual media consumers are in focus and old sender-recipient models are obsolete. While "push" culture is collective, slow-paced, closed, community-bound, uniform, and based on a paradigm of production, "pull" culture is individual, private, fast-paced, micro-oriented, open, diverse, fragmented, and based on a paradigm of active consumption

The increased spread of information is of great importance for strategic communication since it affects people's attitudes and behavior. The need to make choices based on massive amounts of information from different actors leads to increased uncertainty. Organizations in modernity could rely on history and authority; late modern organizations have to earn their license to operate every day. The competition between organizations of all kinds has increased— there is a lot more choice and a great deal of accessible information for customers and citizens to base their decisions on. To be legitimate—adapted to social and cultural norms—has become more important. Accordingly, strategic communication capabilities have become more relevant than before, used to communicate, negotiate, and shape perceptions of legitimacy between organizations and society. The sociologist Ulrich Beck (1992) argued that there has been a shift from a modern industrial society to a late modern *risk* society. This society means that we are confronted with technological and environmental problems and threats towards us as individuals. The former structure of authority has been replaced with a mandatory requirement to make our own choices, which leads to increased uncertainty. The risk society is an advanced industrial society that systematically produces more and more risks, which in turn will be subject to public conflicts and debates.

The rise of late modern society may be found in the changes in Western society during the 1960s and 1970s and in other parts of the world at other times, leading to new conflicts, environmental awakening, and questioning of the established social and cultural order.

The new technologies have created new opportunities for collective action. Jenkins (2006) points to three key characteristics of the new structure, which all have great relevance for strategic communication. First, he notes that we live in a convergent media culture, where old and new media interact and new forms of communication opens up. The forms and genres that were established during the modern era are still there, but are influenced and slowly changed by new media technologies and formats. Media and communication use is now mobile—we chose, collect and interpret what is going on while on the move. Second, Jenkins point to the emergence of participatory culture. Digital media makes direct feedback possible and sets collective processes in motion beyond the professional actor's domain. Communication that takes place between stakeholders—that is, between participant and participant—becomes more important than information that is spread from senders in a traditional organizational or societal hierarchy. Third, the development strengthens the creation of collective intelligence: problems are resolved through communication with various partners who contribute different parts of what becomes a whole.

5   Organizational identity and culture

Probably the most important part of strategic communication is communication with coworkers. Without internal communication, the conditions do not exist for an organization to exist and operate. Research shows that organizations that develop effective communication systems develop a more positive working environment and achieve their goals more easily (Morley, Shockley-Zalabak, & Cesaria, 2002). This communication enables an organization to achieve the goals of the business. In a general way, the purpose of internal strategic communication is to communicate the objectives and to coordinate the various units, departments, and individuals so that efforts to achieve the goals are synchronized. In addition, strategic communication should work to ensure that the organizational culture and its norms and values are disseminated and anchored among employees. These two communication tasks are at an overall organizational level. Another important task is to secure the communication that is directly linked to the organizational members' everyday work processes.

Three building blocks

Internal communication consists of three building blocks: hierarchical communication, mass communication, and informal communication (Whitworth, 2006). These together constitute an internal communication system (the components are interdependent).

Hierarchical communication

Traditionally, internal communication relies on communication that follows the hierarchical structure; information "moves" to coworkers and from them back up to management, which makes the final decisions for the organization. Industrialist Henri Fayol, father of the classical organizational school of administration, said that information should always go to service. This means that all steps in the organization hierarchy – a set of positions ranged from top to bottom – should be followed to ensure secure communication and unified ordering. An important point of departure in this school is that centralization is a natural act. All impressions are to be gathered in the "brain" (i.e. in management), and from these will come well-thought-out decisions that set the organization in motion towards its goals. Apparently, the administrative school has a fairly rational starting point. For example, it is assumed that managers in the management team can access all information and that they can process and analyze this in order to reach an optimal decision. In theory it might seem logical that members of the management team make the decisions, as they should have a good overview of the organization's activities. However, we all know that decision-making processes are considerably more complex in practice. Despite this, the thinking and practices of the administrative school are still to be found in many organizations.

Historically, this communication mostly involved information disseminated from the top down without any noticeable feedback from coworkers to management. In a small company, this kind of communication can be successful, but the bigger and more complex an organization is, the less likely it will be that such communication works well. An organization with many hierarchical levels also means that the information must take many "steps" before it reaches the final recipient—and there is also a risk that the information will stop on the way to the recipient. Another disadvantage is that this mode of communication is slow because the information can be delayed at one or more of the various levels. A further drawback from an organizational perspective is that communication is highly dependent on the managers' communicative ability and competence. At the same time, many studies show that coworkers prefer to receive information from their immediate boss, experiencing it as more credible than the information that comes directly from management.

Paradoxically, many organizations have been poor at telling managers about their communication responsibilities, giving them training in communication, measuring how well they communicate, and rewarding those who do a good job (Whitworth, 2006). But it's not just about conveying or delivering information to the coworkers "straight up and down." To be effective, it is necessary to adapt the message to the recipient, to give a sense of context, and to communicate it in an engaging way (Simonsson, 2006). In addition, it is vital that managers take on a sorting and interpretation responsibility. Studies here show that coworkers find the amount of information that is prevalent in organizations stressful and time consuming. Managers therefore have an important role sifting information so that coworkers only need to look at what is necessary. But the communication responsibility that is most important, and perhaps also the most difficult, is to help employees interpret the information—to indicate what it means for the department and for each employee. This is about adjusting and translating the message for the recipient. Although the need for message adaptation has for a long time been accepted as obvious in communication studies, it is often unmet in practice. Too commonly, information is distributed to coworkers directly from senior management, whose special interests, fields, knowledge, background, and prioritization obviously affect the message. In addition, many middle managers do not dare interpret information to recipients as they are afraid they will misrepresent the message (Simonsson, 2002).

A particularly important aspect of formal communication is that the managers included in the leadership team are good communicative role models. It makes a very significant difference if they move around the organization and show a willingness to communicate with employees and create a proper dialogue. This practice has been referred to as management by walking around, which coworkers prefer to management by screening around—when managers control and communicate via information and communication technologies such as email and web pages. Top managers actively participate in internal communication at the various hierarchical levels, creating a communication environment that facilitates the flow of information up and down and helps create and maintain trust between employees and management.

Mass media communication

The internal mass media also have an important role in the communication system. Among the more important media are email, web pages, newsletters, staff magazines, and meetings. When mass media were introduced into organizations, they significantly improved control of the timing and consistency of messages compared to reliance on managers as intermediaries (Whitworth, 2006). Initially, journalists were employed to produce the internal publications. The growth of personal newspapers coincided with the emergence of the organizational theory of human relations—from the 1940s onwards. This school can be seen as a reaction to the previously dominant rationalist organizational theory, especially scientific management. One of the human relations school's main points is that people have social needs in their working life; no reasonable financial reward compensates the staff for not enjoying themselves. The researchers behind the school found, among other things, that informal groups were crucial for wellbeing and productivity. Personnel magazines were therefore introduced in many organizations to satisfy their staff's social needs. These newspapers initially focused on reports of corporate celebrations, football tournaments, gold watches, and the like, while reports on the organization's strategies, financial results, products, industry news, and competitors were more unusual. This has now changed. Although the satisfaction of the staff's social needs is still important for the modern personnel newspaper, most of the space is used for reporting on the strengths and weaknesses of the organization.

The backbone of the internal mass media system is now information and communication technology. Since the establishment of internet technology in Western organizations from the mid-1990s, intranets, with web pages and email, have become the primary internal medium. Sweden was probably the country where the intranet was introduced most rapidly. There are several explanations for this, the most important being that internet technology was already present in many organizations. Swedes are also generally interested in technology and historically have been quick to adopt new developments. In addition, the government under former prime minister Carl Bildt ensured that all Swedes would have access to a computer with an internet connection, including through public libraries and so-called personnel purchases (government subventions of computer purchases).

Email is probably the digital medium most used in modern organizations due to its speed, the independence of time and space in communication, and the informal communication style that characterizes most of an organization's internal emails. While email is highly appreciated, it is the medium that contributes most to the information overflow that is a feature of today's organizations. In some organizations, 80–90 percent of email is internal mail. The overflow means that coworkers need to spend more time searching, reading, reviewing, sorting, discarding, and correcting the information. It also means that more time is spent on information management and less time on actual working tasks. According to Heide (2002), the great advantage of the intranet is that it increases access to information, which can contribute, inter alia, to:

- the organization being perceived as more transparent and better understood by its employees.
- the organization becoming more democratic, as employees have both access to information and the opportunity to express their views and convey them to management.
- better conditions for organizational learning.

This all sounds very good, but it also calls into question the amount of time spent on information management and learning (as a result of information management) in relation to carrying out duties. Our experience is that many managers consider that employees spend too much time surfing the intranet and sending emails that are not directly related or relevant to the tasks. It would seem to be a matter of balance: it is important that employees are well informed, but at the same time, not everyone needs to know "everything."

Informal communication

The body of internal communication with the greatest volume is, without competition, informal communication. It is the foundation and pillar for the continuous organizational processes through which an organization is designed and maintained (Mumby, 2011). As mentioned earlier, informal communication complements the formal and fills in the information gaps that exist. Through informal communication, interpretations and meaning-making processes also take place. As soon as employees meet in different contexts—at meetings, in the corridor, at the copier, in the lunchroom, in the training room—different things are discussed regarding the organization. Informal networks exist in all organizations; they cannot be created, initiated, or controlled by management. In the literature these networks are called communities of practice. For example, members can tell each other about problems with the new copy machine, what they think about the new CEO, what the cuts in the subsidiary will mean, and how the competitor's new product might affect the organization's sales. The understanding of individual employees is largely based on informal communication between members of informal networks. Research has also shown that organizational learning primarily takes place through informal communication. Information is transported, new knowledge is produced, and a common knowledge base exists in these networks.

Unfortunately, management groups do not realize the importance of informal communication (or the jungle telegraph, as it is sometimes termed). A common perception is that staff should not stand in the hallway and talk with one another, but rather should remain at their workplaces and carry out their duties. This view in no way brings informal communication to its knees. Communication is moved to other places, not least to email correspondence. However, informal communication can be an important part of strategic communication. The wise communication professional recognizes the benefits and strength of informal communication and utilizes it as an effective tool. The strength of informal communication is that it is cheap and fast and also perceived as reliable since the information is received from people in one's informal network. One way to utilize informal communication is to invite so-called opinion leaders (i.e. informal leaders) to monthly breakfast meetings with the CEO. Issues raised and discussed during these meetings will be spread quickly and efficiently throughout the organization. As they spread, the messages will be adapted to the recipient. At the same time, there is the likelihood of misinterpretation as the message is spiced up and angled—a risk that everyone who has experience of rumors knows. The further a message moves its source, the more it differs from the original.

Examples of informal communication: the police and the pencils

It was confidently believed within a Swedish police area that the regional manager had ordered that pens be gathered in for savings reasons. Each member of the police force should only have two pens. The rumor spread in the corridors and via social media, and employees began to be really upset about the situation. Around this time the police department underwent the most major organizational change in its history and resistance to the changes was immense. There were therefore numerous rumors, many discrediting police officers and managers. The regional police chief began to investigate where and how this persistent rumor had begun. It turned out that the source of the rumor was a messenger. A new government procurement had recently been completed and several suppliers had been replaced, including the supplier of pens. The messenger thought the new supplier's price on pencils too high, and since large savings needed to be made within the police, he asked his colleagues to return pencils they did not use to the storeroom. This then led to rumors that the police chief planned to collect up pencils and limit the number distributed to two per person.

The importance of negative information

There are a very large number of texts that treat downwards information dissemination in an organization – what media should be used, how messages should be designed to get the greatest possible effect, and so forth. However, not much has been written on upward communication or feedback to the management, even though this form of communication is basic to an organization; Tourish and Hargie (2004b) say that an organization without upward communication is like a bird with one wing.

In recent years, an increasing number of researchers have been studying the phenomenon of organizational silence. It arises in organizations characterized by a closed and negative organizational culture that creates a non-democratic atmosphere that tends to silence organizational members' voices. Even the phenomenon of self-censorship has attracted increased interest among researchers. Self-censorship occurs under the same conditions as organizational silence and can be described as witholding important and relevant information for the purpose of protecting oneself (Detert & Edmondson, 2011). The reason why self-censorship occurs is that the organizational climate is perceived as not allowing or inviting the sharing of information (Hayes, Glynn, & Shanahan, 2005). One of the most important social theorists behind the research on organizational silence and self-censorship is the German state scientist Elisabeth Noelle-Neumann (1993), who wrote *The Spiral of Silence*. The silence spiral is a political science theory and mass communication theory that describes how a certain perception becomes dominant and helps keep those who have other perceptions and see themselves as a minority remain silent to avoid isolation from the majority. An important point of departure in the theory is that people are social beings who are afraid of being excluded from the community. In order to become popular, people constantly monitor their surroundings to try to discern the dominant opinion on a particular matter so they can adjust their views to reflect those of the majority.

In early research, silence was interpreted in organizations as loyalty—if no one raised their voice, everything was in order (Shojaie, Matin, & Barani, 2011). Nowadays, researchers emphasize the importance of an organization allowing a variety of different, even contradictory, views (Cheney, Christensen, Zorn, & Ganesh, 2011). In a well-functioning organization, organizers can express their views and point out wrongdoings and mistakes. One form of organization that has come a long way in listening to employees is the so-called high reliability organization (Sutcliffe, 2011). Examples of such organizations are nuclear power plants, aircraft carriers, pharmaceutical companies, and hospitals. Should there be a crisis in such an organization, the consequences might well be disastrous. For this reason there is a focus on errors and mistakes. Employees are encouraged to share negative information in order that the organization learns and is better able to avoid mistakes and possible crises. Unfortunately, there are probably more organizations where zero tolerance for errors is the rule. Research (e.g. Burris, 2012) shows that many managers tend to see coworkers that communicate divergent or negative information as less competent, and such coworkers also tend to receive less support from their closest manager. This of course creates poor conditions for the expression of upward negative information and consolidates a closed communication environment where criticism is not accepted. It is important to have managers that support and encourage employees to give negative upward information. However, Detert and Edmondson (2011) argue that the most important factor is coworkers' experience of earlier attempts to deliver negative information to managers.

It is not only employees who find it difficult to communicate negative information. Even executives can be challenged to produce negative information, such as news of someone's contract being terminated or major organizational change. There is a cowardly tendency among managers to quickly and impersonally communicate negative news via electronic media (Timmerman & Harrison, 2005). This is to distance themselves from those who are affected by the information. A likely outcome is that employees' react to the news even more negatively than they might otherwise. Managers' reluctance to communicate negative information is called the MUM effect. MUM stands for "keep mum about undesirable messages". The effect was discovered in a study by Rosen and Tesser (Rosen & Tesser, 1970, p. 253), who state: "The reluctance to transmit information is directly dependent on the inferred desirability of the message for the potential recipient." The MUM effect occurs when sending out negative information is avoided by delaying communication, delegating responsibility for communicating the message, or modifying the original information. The result may be that the organizational climate is characterized by suspicion and employees feel nervous and insecure about the situation in the organization.

Managers who need to communicate negative information may also choose to distance themselves from those affected by the information. These managers simply avoid the unpleasant interpersonal situations that can occur if they "walk around" and switch to the screening around style of management—to carrying out their leadership role through, for example, email (Peters, 1992). Leadership of this sort is rarely appreciated by employees, who want to meet their boss and be seen and affirmed. If the manager uses email to deliver negative information, there is a high risk that employees will become dispirited and unmotivated and lose confidence in both the manager and the organization. Leadership and communication are closely related to each other. Most leadership involves some form of communication. It is correctly said that leadership is impossible without communication (Clifton, 2015).

In this context it may be interesting to address the concept of interactions law (Bies & Shapiro, 1988). This can be defined as the quality of the interpersonal treatment that people experience in organizational contexts. Interaction law has two components: information law and interpersonal justice. The first is about how well the organization can answer questions like "Why?" and "Why me?" These are the questions that people at the receiving end of negative information often ask themselves. Employee acceptance of a decision is improved if the organization's explanations are timely and sufficiently detailed. The latter—interpersonal justice—deals with the extent to which individuals are treated with respect in communications.

Furthermore, it is important to consider the choice of medium when managers communicate negative information. An explanation is more likely to be successful if the medium enables social clues, such as emotional intensity and non-verbal behavior. In other words, information law is easier to achieve with "richer" media, such as face-to-face communication and video and telephone conferencing, than with "poorer" media such as email and formal documents. At the same time, it should be noted that poorer media can also have their advantages: because written communication is not synchronous, the sender has time to formulate the text with care and choose the most appropriate words. Written communication also makes it possible to be more detailed than is usually possible in verbal communication.

In the case of complex information, the best media channel could be a combination of a poorer medium, such as email, and a richer medium like face-to-face communication. For example, a manager could first meet with the affected staff, give them the information, and try to answer their questions. At the meeting they could be given documents providing more in-depth information. At a later date, the boss could meet again with the employees, who probably have more questions to ask. Treating employees with respect creates a better basis for the successful communication of negative information.

Employees as ambassadors

In recent years, research has increasingly focused on organizational members, usually coworkers, and the importance of creating, enhancing, and reproducing the organization's brand and identity through their everyday actions. The coworkers are undoubtedly the most important messengers, even in optimal cases the organization's top ambassadors (Hatch & Schultz, 2010; Heide & Simonsson, 2011). For instance, in service meetings between customers and staff in a shop, the customers' perceptions of the organization are communicated, maintained, or changed. Unfortunately, many organizations neglect or simply do not realize the value of "walking the talk" and "living the brand" (Karmark, 2005). There must be a clear link between organizations' strategic vision and communication, and this requires greater communicative awareness and skills in many management teams.

In practice, however, it is often simply that the management team does not pay enough attention to embedding new messages, thoughts, norms, and values in the workforce. Mitchell (2004) emphasizes that the real challenge is helping employees understand how new words may be translated into action. Even the vaguest brand descriptors, such as "friendly" and "helpful", must be translated into everyday life experiences. The coworkers themselves must carry out this process, supported by their immediate boss, because it is the quality of the coworkers' daily work that reflects what the brand and organization really stands for. For example, the Swedish telecom company Telia had problems transitioning from state-owned Televerket, with its not very service-intensive focus, to the service-oriented practice of the new company. During this transition, large amounts of money were spent on new logos, signs, and business interiors to convey the intended message of the leadership behind the Telia brand through market communication. However, the management forgot to make sure that the coworkers understood how the new values might be translated into practice. This meant that customers met staff who acted and thought as they had under Televerket.

From a communicative and opinion-making perspective, it is crucial that employees discuss with each other and those responsible for change for a common understanding. The risk otherwise is that the values of the brand will only be a matter of lip service, something that employees can possibly recite when asked but lacking any real influence on their thinking or actions.

A common problem in many organizations facing change is that management is in a hurry—it wants to see an effect as quickly as possible. One consequence may be that persistent persuasion programs are launched, with different media and intermediaries used to give the board, for instance, a speedy result. But change processes take time, and it is also an open question to what extent it is possible to persuade employees to embrace a new identity or change their values. With regard to a change in an organization's brand, it is commonplace that a market mindset, which has penetrated most Swedish organizations since the 1980s, takes over, placing the emphasis on consumers. One consequence of this is "campaign syndrome", in which those responsible for the brand see different types of market campaign as the primary way of expressing the brand's identity and values (Schultz, 2005). An explanation for this syndrome may be that those responsible are seduced by the idea that their message might appear in the media.

A concept that is relevant in this context, which characterizes a large part of strategic communication, is *autocommunication* (Broms & Gahmberg, 1983; Cheney & Christensen, 2001a). This is communication that is directed at target groups outside the organization, but whose message is more meaningful to and really targeted at employees and sender. Christensen and Cheney (2000) point out that organizations have a need to remind themselves what they are and what it is that unites them by using different symbols, values, and terms. The same applies to all people, groups, cultures, and communities: all need to communicate in order to clarify for themselves and others who they are and what they stand for (Geertz, 1973). Autocommunication can thus resemble a diary, whose purpose is to shape and clarify an individual's thoughts. For example, organizations' websites, annual reports, organizational history books, job listings, identity programs, editorial material in news-papers, advertising for the organization's products/services, and the archi-tectural design of the organization's buildings may be seen as autocommunication. Autocommunication is often used unconsciously by organizations, but there are also examples of conscious usage. For instance, the communications department of Siba, a large Swedish home electronics store, worked on autocommunication as a strategy. In 2004, it showed commercials on TV4 in which employees of the company presented price-discounted pro-ducts and talked to the audience about what characterizes Siba as a company. The movies were recorded with a handheld camera and the "shakiness" and a certain graininess in the films enhanced the sense of authenticity. Coworkers saw the commercials and were of course particularly interested when a famil-iar colleague made an appearance. The message about the company's particular characteristics was likely to have had a greater impact on employees than on consumers, and these commercials were part of the organization's efforts to strengthen employee identification with the company. The power of auto-communication is that external media have higher status and more credibility than traditional internal media.

Transmission communication is alive!

There are clear signs that communication is increasingly being discussed within organizations and that communication issues are now higher on the management agenda. Astra Zeneca is an example of a company that takes communication seriously. A major change in production began in 2006, with the goal of transitioning to lean production. Contrary to the usual situation in most other organizations during change phases, the communication depart-ment was driving the process from the beginning, contributing expertise and a communication perspective.

Unfortunately, it is rare that organizations look at things from a commu-nication perspective at times of crisis or change. More often, they adopt a linear transmission view of communication—"information is spreading", "the message is to reach out to all employees"—and if the message fails to reach home, the information is sent out again, possibly in modified form or through another medium.

In the merger of certain Nordic banks that became the new major bank Nordea, a "cascade technique" was used; this meant having information about the new corporate culture "spill out" and "flow down from the pipeline" to all employees (Søderberg & Vaara, 2003). The information was spread through different media and fora to all employees, and the idea was—of course—that employees would receive, understand, accept, and internalize the new culture. Christensen and Cheney (2000) argue that it is strange that so many organi-zations still believe in controlled messages that can be spread top down and assume that a message is received directly and "owned" by the recipients. This attitude persists despite the fact that modern management is generally aware of the existence of multiple identities and the advantage of strategic diversity. But when it comes to formulating the organization's vision and mission in times of change, management is usually not interested in allowing employees a free interpretive hand. Instead, both consultants and management are devoted to "giving" the organizational members the exact meaning of the vision and mission (Christensen & Cheney, 2000).

What communication strategies are used?

Research shows that organizations' communication strategies are often based on existing practices – along with some thoughtful activities. A review of a large number of communication systems and literature in the field indicates that there are five typical strategies (Clampitt, DeKoch, & Cashman, 2000):

- *Spray and pray.* This strategy means that management "spray" employees with all sorts of information, the assumption being that employees are competent to distinguish between important and unimportant information. The argument would seem to be that if employees have ample information they can make better decisions. The strategy is thus based on a rationalistic mindset that believes that people have an unlimited ability to receive information and then analyze it to make optimal decisions.
- *Tell and sell.* Using this strategy, members of the organization get slightly less information. Management only communicates what it believes has to do with the organization's core business. The first step in the strategy is that management identifies the important points; in the second step it tries to "sell" its view of these matters. Leaders who follow this strategy spend a lot of energy on beautiful presentations but rarely care about having a meaningful discussion with their employees. Feedback from employees is also not seen as particularly important. It seems that here management is convinced it knows best.
- *Underline and investigate.* Here, management presents some main ideas, which it then lets employees discuss and reflect on. The management shows confidence in the employees and their opinions are assumed to be relevant to the organization's development. The basic attitude of management is to listen to employees in order to find out if there are any misunderstandings or obstacles.
- *Identify and respond.* In this strategy, the employees are at the center, emphasizing the importance of learning about and understanding opinion in a complex reality. This strategy is defensive: the management tries to identify the employees' concerns, then answer them. Here it is the employees who set the agenda, while management responds to, for example, rumors, hints, and leaks. Unlike in the previous strategy, the attitude here is that employees know best what factors critically affect the organization.

- *Withhold and defend.* Management teams using this strategy wait to inform employees until their hand is forced. Managers assume that information is power, and they do not want to share this power. Another common assumption is that employees cannot grasp the entire picture and therefore they should not be given any more information than necessary.

In practice, several strategies—or hybrids of them—can be used at the same time, but the tendency is for members of the organization to get either, at one extreme, all the information ("spray and pray") or at the other, almost no information ("withhold and defend"). Both extremes, however, give employees the same basic problem: it is hard to understand what is happening in and around the organization, and the creation of meaning becomes problematic.

Some advice …

Finally, we want to provide some advice on how to improve internal communication. Management groups and the rest of the workforce sometimes seem to exist on different planets: there is a large gap between them, which of course makes effective communication difficult. Communication researchers Owen Hargie and Dennis Tourish (2004) believe that many communication efforts resemble messages that are pushed off like missiles from a central command bridge. But there is usually no control of the missile and no possibility of controlling the effect of the launch. Another problem is that the communication aspect is rarely part of strategic decisions, despite clear evidence that effective communication is a prerequisite for successful activities (Clampitt et al., 2000). Hargie and Tourish (2004) argue that organizational communication needs to be thoroughly evaluated in order for it to evolve. They have reviewed a large number of evaluations and found four themes, which can also be considered as concrete advice for improving internal communication:

- *Employees prefer information from the nearest boss!* The closest boss has particular importance for communication efficiency. It is therefore key to provide managers with communication support and continuous communication training.
- *Retrieve employee opinions continuously!* Create an environment where employees are treated as important actors and not as hired workers. Information should be spread throughout the organization. The more "secrets" that exist, the less trust employees will have in management and managers. Organization members want to be informed. Using a *mushroom management strategy* ("Keep them in the dark, feed them shit and watch them grow") with employees is unwise. A consequence of poorly functioning formal communication is that informal communication

increases dramatically to fill the information vacuum that occurs. Shockley-Zalabak and Ellis (2000) write: "The reception desk has a stronger relation to effectiveness and job satisfaction than other measured communication activities."

- *Face-to-face channels should be used at maximum*! Despite all the sophisticated digital media available, research shows that we prefer face-to-face contact with people (Heide, 2002).
- *Employees value communication training!* It seems that organizations have not sufficiently recognized the importance of training their members in the organization's communication skills.

6   Change and crisis communication

Organizational changes and crises are topics of daily discussion for most organizations. The increased media coverage of societal crises, which can be everything from natural disasters to political change, places a high demand on public authorities and other actors for faster and more effective communicative action. In short, crises, which can be defined as critical turning points (or crucial events), are increasing the need for strategic communication (Frandsen & Johansen, 2017). In this chapter we will cover change communication and crisis communication, two increasingly important fields of practice for communicators. Recent research (e.g. Maitlis & Christianson, 2014; Maitlis & Sonenshein, 2010) has also shown that there is a close connection between change communication and crisis communication. This close connection has contributed to the development and growth of internal crisis communications (Heide, 2013; Heide & Simonsson, 2015).

Organizational changes

It is said that we live in a dynamic and ever-changing world. Though change is not unique to our time, globalization, hardening competition, increased travel, climate change, consumer preferences, and the increased spread and use of diverse information and communication techniques (ICT) have created a very particular world for many. Just like previous generations, we see our time as one of great uncertainty and subversion (Alvesson & Sveningsson, 2016).

Researchers have long been interested in organizational change. The first article that focused specifically on this field was published in the journal *Human Relations* at the end of the 1940s, and the recommendations made by the authors Coch and French (1948) are not so different from what is said today (e.g. Barratt-Pugh, Bahn, & Gakere, 2013; Smollan, 2013). They contended that organizational change should be implemented even if those affected initially feel hesitant about it; the most important thing is to effectively communicate why change is needed and include the affected parties in change implementation. Today, we often see organizational change as constructive: the more, the better.

Organizational change is one type of response to pressures or forces. According to Ford and Ford (1995), the core of organizational change is difference in conditions, states, or moments of time. This understanding of organizational change takes for granted that a normal, stable state exists. However, in practice organizations are continuously changing (Weick, Sutcliffe, & Obstfeld, 2005).

Why does change happen so often in today's organizations? One answer is that organizations tend to homogenize; they do not want to differ too much from each another and therefore standardize. Powell and DiMaggio (1991) describe this homogenization tendency as isomorphism. One form of homogenization is *cognitive isomorphism*: this describes the tendency of individuals who do not know how to handle a certain situation to look at and imitate the behaviour of others in a similar situation. For example, if the benefits of knowledge management are vaunted in journals and at various conferences, managers may see this as a feasible way to solve a lack of innovation among their organization members.

Another form is *normative isomorphism*, which describes responding to external pressure to appear moral and well adjusted. This can be seen when organizations avoid differentiating themselves from the majority of other organizations in the field. This can be seen in the recent popularity of CSR (corporate social responsibility). When multinational corporations such as H&M, Ikea and McDonald's constantly talk about taking social responsibility and have clear codes of conduct, other organizations begin to feel a normative pressure to follow suit and adopt CSR principles. Mats Alvesson (2013) argues that isomorphism's activities and consequences are "shop-window dressing", meaning that they simply look good from the outside. Such display window events rarely have any real impact on core business activities, but they give external stakeholders such as shareholders, politicians, environmental groups, and journalists the impression that the organization is prosperous, acts ethically, takes care of its employees, is financially competent, and so on. In this context, brand, image, and illusions are very important. Many managers are now jumping on the bandwagon of new management trends such as lean management and knowledge management.

In every organization two forces coexist – one force preserves, which Schon (1973) calls dynamic conservatism, and the other force wants to adapt to different forms of change. These forces challenge all change initiatives. Those who are responsible for organizational changes must consequently identify and embrace the two forces in order to appropriately adapt the strategic communication.

Dismal and disappointing outcomes

Organizational change often results in disappointing outcomes. Research shows that many organizational changes do not actually go very far and have very small effects on business (Alvesson, 2013). It is common to claim that as much as 70 percent of all major planned organizational change efforts fail (Beer & Nohria, 2000; Burke, 2011; Kotter & Schlesinger, 2008). However, this figure should not be taken as a given. Hughes (2011) analyzed four key articles that introduced and maintained this particular percentage view. Hughes concludes that 70 percent of all changes do not fail and that the figure is part of a produced narrative unsupported by empirical evidence.

Many organizational changes are set in motion without first conducting a necessity analysis and are thus based on relatively flimsy grounds. This is particularly evident in information and communication technologies (ICT), which were introduced on a broad front in the form of internet and intranets in many Western organizations in the mid-1990s. Historically, we have placed great confidence in new technologies and in media such as the telegraph, radio, telephone, and television; there has been a tendency to hope that these media could reduce distances and strengthen ties both between and within nations, enhance democratic processes, and reduce the risk of war. These media forms have also been linked to increased citizen learning: it is often envisioned that they could raise the general knowledge level of a country, for instance via mobile courses. The same confidence has been placed in the potential of ICTs to improve and streamline learning within organizations (Heide, 2002).

Despite the many capabilities of new media and ICTs, such as the shrinking of time and space, they do not in and of themselves improve the efficiency of human learning. Learning processes are complex and cannot be tackled by media alone. Understandably, the great confidence we have placed in ICTs has led business leaders in many countries to invest heavily in new media, often with marginal benefits (Sveiby, 1997).

Blasé personnel

Members of many contemporary organizations have experienced rule-bound organizational changes, which have rarely made any difference to how business is conducted. One of the authors has worked as a consultant for a Swedish car company, where the interviewees testified in a survey that they expected a major organizational change to occur every second year. Over time, these employees became jaded: they knew that it was not worth their while to commit in any real way to an organizational change as another would soon follow. Simply put, it would waste too many staff resources to get involved. At the time of the survey the organization was undergoing a change that placed the company's engineers in different teams. One interviewee said that management had given each team a new name and placed this name on a sign above the door to the department, but these names lacked practical significance for employees; they already had informal networks and there was a strong unofficial organization within the company that guided their daily work. As a result, the employees continued to work as they had always done, ignoring the changes. The same interviewee also said that employees recognized that organizational change usually came either from management following a new management trend or from some sort of change in management prompting new leaders to assert their new leadership role.

These frequent organizational changes create a BOHICA – Bend Over, Here It Comes Again – mentality. Seasoned employees learn over time that the changes rarely go anywhere and that the most effective way to handle them is to continue with business as usual via informal networks, endeavouring as far as possible not to be affected (Alvesson, 2013). Alvesson stresses that change-happy managers and change-sceptic employees do not make a good equation. In such a situation, it is most likely that constant change initiatives increase distrust of the leadership.

Downsizing and lean management

Downsizing, or the slimming down of an organization in order to engage in "core business", is a management trend that has persisted since the late 1980s. In practice, downsizing means removing all the side and support branches of an organization. This trend has been amplified by the development of new technologies, which have allowed businesses to retain even fewer employees and still operate. The consequence has been slim, downright anorexic, organizations. A major problem with these cutbacks is that the strategy is only effective in the short term and in stable conditions.

Although there is clear evidence that organizations are suffering financially by cutting back in this way and that long-term profits are reduced by cutbacks, the trend of downsizing and lean management has continued (Tourish & Hargie, 2004a), with several examples of companies that have downsized immensely. But why do these cuts continue? Irrational leadership is one possible explanation. There are several factors that explain this behaviour, many of them related to communication (Tourish & Hargie, 2004a):

- *Behaviour that is rewarded is carried out.* Research has shown that managers who implement cuts are rewarded, even if the cuts do not result in greater profits and efficiency. Organizations that cut down operations are often seen as more innovative and ranked higher in terms of the quality of their leadership.
- *Illusions about leadership.* There are many misconceptions of leadership as a machine that constantly changes and regenerates. Business and finance newspapers typically describe managers as individuals with power and control. Consequentially, newly appointed managers typically want to display their leadership and show that they have control over the organization. The fastest way to do this is to cut down operations and therefore operational costs, as opposed to building relations, communicating, and understanding the organization, which is a lengthy and difficult undertaking.
- *Self-rationalizing stories.* Managers often try to create different rational stories that legitimate and justify their actions. These stories can be so compelling that the managers themselves become seduced by their own rhetoric.

- *Lack of critical feedback.* It is difficult for management to get critical feedback on the impact of their decisions.
- *Prioritizing short-term relationships.* In terms of personal career development, it is most advantageous to be employed by several organizations, increase your salary, and gain more experience and a wider network. As a result, many managers choose to demonstrate their ability to act quickly on their own for the sake of short-term gains, instead of thinking of long-term organizational interests.
- *Irrationality.* The trend of organizational cuts can be based on the assumption that the decisions of management must be rational and well thought out. This is not necessarily the case. Management very often follows the example of other organizations and makes similarly unreflexive decisions (see above for isomorphism).

The above list clearly shows that there is much to do in terms of leaders' understanding of the change process. Communication is an integral part of this process.

Communicating changes

Communication is vital to successful organizational change and downsizing (Johansson & Heide, 2008; Lewis, 2011). An organizational change is, in essence, an act of communication (Jian, 2011). However, despite the growing literature in recent years that takes a communications perspective on change, the importance of communication during changes often goes unnoticed by both practitioners and researchers (Lewis, 2014). Actors in organizations tend to take a too simple and unreflexive view on communicating change; managers assume that if employees are given only positive information about the change, then they will simply go along with it.

Lewin's (1951) classic model of change is still in use today, though it is now well past its sell-by date. According to this model, static and "frozen" organizations need to be "thawed" before change can be implemented. When the changes are in place, the organizations will refreeze in a new static state. The popularity of this model can presumably be attributed to the picture it paints of change as a linear and thus fully controllable process. Very little research has criticized Lewin's model for failing to consider that change can itself change over time, that goals can shift, or that there is a dynamic between change and stability (Lewis, 2011).

In the run-up to change it is vital that staff are given clear information as to why the change is necessary, all employees are treated with dignity, and fair and transparent procedures are used (Tourish & Hargie, 2004a), otherwise it may be difficult to maintain trust amongst the employees who stay with the organization after the change. To maintain the confidence of employees it is vital to increase the flow of information during the change process. When cuts are underway and employees don't know who will be laid off, rumours spread to fill the information void created by insufficient formal communication. This can be explained by the theory of meaning: the natural tendency and desire of humans to create understanding and meaning in times of uncertainty.

One difficulty surrounding communicating personnel cuts is that employees know that cuts one year tend to mean further cuts the next year. In other words, the "psychological contract" between management and employees is tarnished. Another difficulty is that managers often both underestimate the amount of information that employees want and need and overestimate the amount of information that they are providing (Tourish & Hargie, 2004a). It is also important that managers themselves model the new practices and values that the change requires (Barratt-Pugh et al., 2013). Change communication is extremely difficult, but it is key to success. Communications should, like crisis communications (discussed below), be frequent, consistent (i.e. not contradictory), and open. Above all, it is essential that everyone involved in the change understands that it will take an extremely long time to reach the desired result.

Crisis communication

Over the past few decades, crises have been given more and more attention by the media. There are intense reports on various types of personal crisis, such as accidents, divorces, and illnesses, and also on the effects of war and natural disasters on different societies and countries. However, it is organizational crises that have received the most attention. According to Mitroff (2001, p. 5): "crises are no longer an aberrant, rare, random, or peripheral feature of today's society. They are all built into the very fabric and fiber of modern societies." A couple of years ago one of the biggest public authorities in Sweden, the Employment Service, had just entered a period of crisis. Confidence in the authority's management was quite low and the impact of recently implemented labor market measures were under question. However, after media exposure of the director general's high cell-phone bills, public pressure increased rapidly. The crisis escalated and the government acted quickly by dismissing the director general. However, the damage had been done and a debate around the future of the Employment Service began. Though the actions of the director general contributed to the government's rapid intervention, the main reason was that the organization already had weak credibility, thus intensifying the seriousness of the crisis.

Since the new millennium, the mass media has been saturated by scandals, such as those associated with the directors of the American energy enterprise Enron (2001) and the Swedish insurance company Skandia (2003). In both cases, the scandals had grave consequences for both the companies themselves and the directors, whose actions led to tough and lengthy legal repercussions. Enron went through a complicated bankruptcy process and sold the last part of its enterprise in 2006, while Skandia has had to work extremely hard to try to get back its previously favorable position in the public eye.

So, what is an organizational crisis? There are of course many definitions in the literature. One of the most common is proposed by Lerbinger (1997): "An event that brings, or has the potential for bringing, an organization into disrepute and imperils its future profitability, growth, and possibly its very survival" (p. 4). This definition suggests that a crisis is something purely negative that could even threaten an organization's ability to survive. A more modern and complex definition is the following by Ulmer, Sellnow and Seeger (2007): "An organizational crisis is a specific, unexpected, and non-routine event or series of events that create high levels of uncertainty and threaten or are perceived to threaten an organization's high-priority goals" (p. 7). This definition embraces the interpretation perspective by pointing out the uncertainty that always arises in organizations that face a crisis. Further, it is noted that a crisis is both an unexpected and a rare event. Contemporary researchers such as Coombs (2015) emphasize that an organizational crisis is not some sort of object that can be found "out there". Rather, an organizational crisis is the perception of an unexpected event that threatens the important expectations of stakeholders. Already two decades ago, Bland (1998, p. 15) stated that "A crisis is not what has happened, it is what people think has happened."

Crisis management as a research field has existed since the 1980s and has generated a large number of texts, models, and theories. The field has sparked the interest of researchers from a number of disciplines, such as business, sociology, psychology, and media and communications. A large part of the research in crisis communication uses the methods that are typically used in the natural sciences. The goal of this research is to find patterns in data that can effectively describe, explain, and predict; most of the research is descriptive and prescriptive and offers various recommendations to organizations. The research is based in large part on successful cases and practitioners' experience. One of the most prominent crisis communication researchers, Timothy Coombs (2006), believes that the field needs to be more broadly developed and more widely based on research that can describe how and why these recommendations are effective. An evident pattern is that most research in crisis communication is focused on external crisis communication – that is, organizations' communications to such external stakeholders such as customers, politicians, journalists, and neighbors. Hence, one of the most important groups, namely coworkers, are more or less ignored in both research and practice. This can be explained by among other things the fact that the majority of researchers within crisis communication have a background in public relations. In *The Handbook of Crisis Communication*, Taylor (2010) underlined that more research must focus on internal aspects if the field of crisis communication is to develop. Since then there has been an increasing amount of research on internal crisis communication, i.e. information, communication and sensemaking among organizational members during the acute phase of a crisis, and also on the intrinsic role of communication in crisis preparedness, anticipation, and learning within an organization (Heide & Simonsson, 2014, 2015).

Crisis researchers often stress that organizations should strive towards "truth" and tell the public exactly what has happened. One of the most frequent recommendations for organizations that have landed themselves in a crisis is, "Tell it all and tell it fast" (Arpan & Roskos-Ewoldsen, 2005, p. 425). To put it bluntly, one could say that effective crisis communication means first deciding what has actually happened and then describing and explaining the event clearly, with absolute transparency and unequivocal language (Tyler, 2005).

Form and content

When it comes to research on organizations' reactions to crises, there are two different specializations: form and content. Form describes what should be done, while content describes what is said in the messages coming from an organization in crisis.

An analysis of the literature in this field has shown that, typically, there are three different recommendations:

- *React quickly!* An organization should give out information about what has happened to all its stakeholders—workers, stockholders, clients, journalists, the public, politicians, and the like—as rapidly as possible. The objective is to fill any informational void that is created when a crisis occurs. If organizations do not provide this information quickly, other actors will fill the void: speculations and rumors will arise. The organization will thus lose control of the situation.
- *Be consistent!* Messages coming from the organization should not contradict each another. Even if different members of the organization speak out after a crisis has occurred, they must deliver a consistent message.
- *Be open!* This is a suggestion that can be interpreted in several ways and it is thus a little controversial. Openness could mean that organizational members are available to give information to interested parties—above all to the mass media. If no such members seem to be available, it can send the message that the organization does not have the crisis under control and is trying to hide something. Openness could also mean that the organization gives out all the information it has to interested parties. However, an organization needs to balance difference interests, as complete openness can have undesirable legal and economic consequences. Nevertheless, researchers agree that full openness is the best way to curate a strong relationship with important interested parties. From an ethical perspective too, full openness is the right path to take.

Content in crisis management has been much more deeply researched than form, and several theories have been developed. The two most common are "corporate apologies" and "image restoration theory".

To apologize means to take responsibility for one's actions; it is a classic rhetorical device. In this focus field of crisis communications, the organization is viewed as an individual who holds various interests. From this perspective there is a very strong reason for organizations to take a personal accountability line when other parties complain about their actions. Researchers in this field have pinpointed various crisis reactions:

- *Denial* – taking no responsibility for the crisis
- *Bolstering* – taking responsibility for the actions, but trying to connect the organization to something positive
- *Differentiating* – trying to separate the crisis from a larger context
- *Transcendence* – placing the crisis in a new, higher context.

One of the lessons from apologia research is that different stakeholders may require different sorts of response to meet their needs during a crisis.

Apologia is the foundation of image restoration theory, which is usually linked with communication researcher William Benoit (2004, 2013), who wrote a great deal about defense strategies. The theory describes organizations' management of situations when they are accused of bad or contentious behavior (Coombs, 2015).

One of the better-known theories, built partly on image restoration strategy, is *situational crisis communication theory*, SCCT (Coombs, 2015). This theory is based on social psychology theory attribution theory, which in this context means that human beings attribute crises to events and other people's behavior in a way that is most beneficial to themselves (Heider, 1958). For example, the reason for a car crash is considered to be the other driver's sloppy behavior rather than one's own lack of attention or care. In SCCT, the crisis analysis takes as its starting point the current situation, assessing how people perceive and relate to a crisis and its causes based on both emotional and cognitive responses. Hence, the theory is based on a categorization of four different clusters (Coombs, 2015):

- The organization is also a victim (attributable to weak responsibility: reputation or trust is barely threatened)—for example, natural disasters, false rumors, workplace violence, tampering with products
- Unfortunate circumstances lie behind the crisis, which was unintentional (the organization accredited with minimal responsibility: moderate threat to reputation or trust)—for example, technical incidents and accidents
- The organization is responsible and could have prevented the crisis (attributable to substantial responsibility: serious threat to reputation or trust)—for example, accidents caused by people (managers, employees) in the form of industrial accidents or products that do damage
- Outrage—for example, fraudulent wrestling, team or rule violation and risk crimes that lead to accidents.

In a second step, it will be determined whether there are aggravating circumstances arising from previous crises and what trust capital (reputation) the organization has had in the past. A defense strategy is then chosen that is appropriate in terms of situation, crisis type, trust capital, and past crisis history. These strategies are similar to those found in Benoit's image repair theory, although Coombs (2015, p. 145) divides them into these main categories: a) deny crisis response strategies, b) diminish crisis response strategies, c) rebuild crisis response strategies, and d) bolstering crisis response strategies. Based on SCCT, there is some general advice for crisis communication. This includes:

- Only take actions with instructional (e.g. factual warnings) and adaptive crisis communication (focus on psychological management) in crises where the organization is a victim and has trust capital and no history of previous aggravating crises.
- Make efforts with diminished crisis communication (do not take responsibility) in crises where the organization is a victim or there has been an unintentional accident.
- Make efforts with reconstruction crisis communication (take responsibility) during emergencies that may have been unviable, where the organization's pre-existing trust capital is weak.
- Make efforts with denial of crisis communication when false rumors spread.
- Do not mix denial with diminishing or rebuilding crisis communication strategies.

Control and prediction

Crisis communications research is typically conducted from a leadership perspective, with the aim of returning the organizational image back to "normal" or how it was before the crisis. Control is therefore the keyword for most researchers in this field. There are many examples of this, especially given the increasingly complex, fast-changing, and unpredictable nature of our world. Christensen (2005) posits that organizations are constantly trying to find new "tools" with which to control the outside world. However, it is unclear whether this sort of control is even possible.

The most usual themes in crisis research are planning, prediction, and control. Planning consists primarily of gathering information. Research shows that organizations typically take in large amounts of information but do not in practice have the capacity to handle, interpret, and analyze the information (Cheney & Christensen, 2001a). This is due to both people's limited cognitive ability and the "filter" that is created by a too-homogeneous management, which tends to see and hear the same thing while missing other perspectives (Sutcliffe, 2001). Despite these obstacles, it is considered particularly important to continuously implement business intelligence and have effective communication channels in place so that changes and difficulties can be quickly reported to management, which will then make good decisions. The basic idea here is that an "early warning system" can prevent or mitigate the effects of a crisis.

However, some researchers, such as Gilpin and Murphy (2006), do not adhere to this idea, believing that this form of planning limits the organization's view instead of expanding it. Planning and preparing for crises is in effect an attempt to reduce ambiguity and uncertainty, which Weick (1995) calls *equivocality*—planning and preparing makes the world seem more controllable. However, the problem with this approach is that it creates the risk of ignoring a large number of factors that can create or contribute to a crisis. The crisis communication researcher Murphy (1996) claims that attempts to control and predict complicated events are meaningless since this is a more or less impossible undertaking. She means that as crises are complex and usually only increase in their complexity over time, it does not serve organizations well to take a reductionist approach.

In contrast to more traditional perspectives, complexity theory does not seek to eliminate and control the ambiguities, paradoxes, and uncertainties of a crisis but rather accepts them as inevitable in the modern world. This theory has been popular in the field of management since the early 1990s. It criticizes the view of organizations as static systems and highlights chaos as a tool to point out the shortcomings of modern management theory. The basis of complexity theory is that constant change is part of the organizational life cycle. Organizations are perceived as self-organizing devices that continuously sense external pressures to change in relation to their environment (Kennan & Hazleton, 2006). This environment is extremely complex, impossible to grasp, explain, or predict, and requires an immediate response from organizations if they are to survive in an increasingly competitive marketplace. The theory thus takes as given that the future is impossible to predict and stability is impossible to achieve in a constantly changing world. Uncertainty and ambiguity are seen as qualities that can help an organization adapt to circumstances it cannot control (Gilpin & Murphy, 2006). Organizations are seen not as strictly governed by rules but as dynamic and constantly changing.

Organizations that accept the complexity of their environment tend to develop four types of behavior (Gilpin & Murphy, 2006):

- Collecting information about their characteristics, environment, stakeholders, and conditions.
- Identifying and stimulating multiple, and sometimes conflicting, organizational goals.
- Emphasis on and encouragement of several close relationships, both internally and externally. These are used to interpret and analyze information and gather new information and produce new knowledge.
- Self-organization and activation of new measures as a result of the newly gathered information and created knowledge.

Most often, and this is the recommended path in most management training, organizations strive to reduce the complexity of a situation instead of
trying to absorb it. They place emphasis on trying to create order in a chaotic
world by attempting to simplify internal structures, minimize goals, formalize
and centralize decision-making, and strive for a state of equilibrium. The
problem with planning and prediction is that organizations tend to lock
themselves into certain rules and procedures and consequentially may fail to
absorb and react to unplanned information or make unexpected decisions
beyond what has been prepared and planned. While complexity absorption is
difficult to implement, research shows that this strategy is the most successful
in turbulent environments.

Furthermore, it can be argued that both a confident, well-planned attitude
and an extremely uncertain attitude can get in the way of what an organization needs most in a dynamic time: openness and curiosity (Weick, 1993).
Being open and curious is necessary for management to develop understanding and create meaning during a crisis and therefore be able to make
appropriate decisions. Preconceived expectations often act as self-fulfilling
prophecies and communication specialists therefore need to work with continuously challenging expectations and consider the implications of the
unexpected.

Handling a changing and complex world

The research fields of change communication and crisis communication both
aim to reduce complexity in various situations. One way to do this is to see
the situation in definite steps, such as Kotter's (1996) eight-step model for
how to successfully manage change and Fink's (1986) four-step model that
describes and explains a crisis. An additional characteristic that is shared by
both research fields is the tendency of the literature to take a management
perspective and use the natural-science theoretical research model. This model
seeks to describe, explain, and predict reality by collecting large amounts of
data. This research method offers elegant linear models (with flow charts and
arrows), which are subsequently widely used among practitioners and teachers. While these models do offer transparency and simplicity, they fall short
in their attempt to fit a complex reality into a simple box. The problem here
is that the myth of organizational rationality is amplified and reproduced,
whereas the reality of most organizations is complex and dynamic.

There is, however, an alternative to these reductionist and simplified-effect
models. Karl E. Weick, whose theories were discussed above, offers a suggestion for how organizations can handle their complex environments. Weick
(1979) posits that organizations themselves need to become more complex in
order to solve complex problems. He speaks about *requisite variety* (originally
introduced by Ross Ashby, 1956), which is the necessity for variety within an
organization: in order to handle complex situations such as crises, organizations need to have a more varied perspective and through this develop a more

nuanced and grounded picture of reality. Organizations can achieve this through more heterogeneous leadership groups: in contrast to the homogenous leadership tradition, organizations tend to thrive more with leadership that represents different genders, age groups, backgrounds, educations, interests, and perspectives. Weick (1988) describes the strength of such heterogeneity as follows: "People can see only those categories and assumptions that they store in cause maps built up from previous experience. If those cause maps are varied and rich, people should see more, and good institutional memory would be an asset" (p. 312).

The law of requisite variety says that diversity within a system must be proportional to the diversity of the environment in which it is trying to fit. Weick claims that if organizations use only simple processes and models to handle complicated information, then only a small amount of the information will be registered, paid proper attention, and interpreted. The result will be that the organization cannot answer the question, "What is going on?" There are only three ways to handle requisite variety (Weick, 1979):

- *Handle variety on a one-to-one basis*. In practice this would mean that one person handles each of the possible factors in an environment and does not deal with anything else. Apart from this being an extremely expensive solution, it would be extremely difficult to grasp, coordinate, and deal with all the information.
- *Decrease variety*. This is a solution that only the most powerful organizations in particular societies can use—for example, through secret networks between big organizations, cartels, and, monopolies.
- *Increase the complexity of the "watcher" taking in information*. This solution increases the watcher's sensitivity regarding variance in the information they are gathering. This person should be able to sense changes in the larger context and choose which information can be ignored, what will not change in the near future, and what is most likely to happen. Through this selection process, the watcher can expand the diversity of their control; they can take in more information and see details that others may miss.

Using any of the above-listed solutions is logistically difficult, can give rise to higher operational costs, and takes time to implement. However, Weick still posits that more complex organizations are better equipped to handle complex environments.

There are several factors that affect the extent to which people within an organization notice what happens around them and subsequently take action based on their interpretation of these events. Three of the most important factors according to Huber and Daft (1987) are:

- *Information load*. This is the complex combination of informational quantity, ambiguity, and variance that needs to be dealt with. When the information load increases, some information typically gets neglected. People then tend to start using different strategies to deal with this neglect, such as increasing their tolerance for mistakes and errors, ranking and filtering information, using multiple medias, or fleeing (Weick, 1995).

- *Informational complexity.* The complexity of the information affects how people interpret and understand it; as complexity increases, so does the ambiguity that people within organizations experience, as they are dealing with a larger number of diverse informational elements (Weick, 1995). Increased informational complexity means that people begin to look for and rely on routine solutions. However, these solutions tend to lead to both misinterpretations and mistakes.
- *Turbulence.* This is a combination of instability and chance. Research has shown that as turbulence increases, so does the use of intuition and heuristics in an organization.

Language is vital for us to perceive the things, nuances, and events that enable us to think abstractly. The significance of language in shaping the understandings and thoughts of individuals was first stressed in the 1920s by the Russian researcher Lev Vygotsky (1978). Vygotsky asserted that children are not able to think in abstract terms before they have learnt a language: language makes it possible for us to be reflexive, and a deeper language makes it possible to reflect more deeply. Weick (1995, p. 12) expresses this in the following manner: "How can I know what I think until I see what I say?" The labels that we place on various phenomena greatly affect how we handle these phenomena. For example, if we say that something is a problem instead of a possibility, we fix both for ourselves and for others the "problem" *as* a problem. "Problem" tends to be a self-fulfilling prophecy as we respond to the event according to its label. The more diversity an organization faces, the greater the likelihood is that we perceive there to be one "right way" and that we develop specific solutions to understand what is happening.

Weick differentiates between *uncertainty*, which can be handled with more information, and *ambiguity*. The latter requires clear values, priorities, and clarity regarding what is important in order for employees to collectively arrive at a new understanding of the situation. In ambiguous situations there are no clear or prepared answers to the questions people have. In a crisis we tend to end up in ambiguous situations, not understanding what is happening or how everything is coming together. Weick (1993) calls this a "cosmological episode," when we perceive the universe to be an irrational and unordered system; he claims that a cosmological period feels like *vu jàde* (French for "never seen"—the opposite of déjà vu, "already seen"): "I have never been here before, I have no idea where I am and no idea who can help me." In situations pervaded by complexity, obscurity, and ambiguity, crisis communications have little value, or as Weick (2001, p. 346) claims: "When you are lost, any old map will do." The most important thing, according to

Weick, is that people begin to act on any interpretation. It is only in retrospect that the event can begin to develop meaning.

Complexity absorption in practice

What then is the best way to absorb and handle complexity in practice? One way is to develop expertise through improvisation. This strategy requires that members of an organization each have a special skill that is valued by management. We usually think of music when we hear the word improvisation—musicians building on a certain pattern to make their own melodies (Falkheimer & Heide, 2010; Weick, 1998). However, in order to be able to improvise, musicians need a sound knowledge and skill base, built through countless hours of practice and training (Falkheimer & Heide, 2010). This is also true in other professional fields. Leaders must thus be sufficiently trained if they are to improvise in different emergency situations, and this training should occur with relative frequency. The need for rapid improvisation and the use of communicators as directors rather than simply transmitters has increased with the emergence of social media.

Another way to handle complexity is to ensure that there is a smooth flow of both positive and negative information within an organization. Insufficient communication, both verbal and non-verbal, is a major contributor to the emergence of crises. When employees feel that something isn't right, it is important that the negative information travels up the organizational hierarchy. There is a clear advantage when trust and openness is widespread among organization members, as this sort of environment provides the best conditions for an organization to get through a time of crisis. During such periods, lateral structures of communication are ideal for uncovering and diagnosing the situation; despite this, organizations typically use vertical structures (Weick, 1990). In an open communications climate, employees talk with one another more often and thus have a better starting point for understanding, meaning creation, learning, and the avoidance or reduction of a crisis. Weick (1990) contends that practitioners in organizations should introduce an important standard: "If things do not make sense, speak up. Only by doing so can you break pluralistic ignorance (i.e. 'you too, I thought I was the only one who didn't know what was going on')" (p. 143).

We typically view crises as an extreme deviation from the norm, though another way to see them is as a natural part of an organization's life cycle. In this case, the goal is not to return to the previous norm; rather, the crisis can be viewed as an opportunity for learning and growth (cf. Stern, 1997). It can therefore be said that part of organizational development and learning is being open to new approaches and ideas and taking advantage of any critical information that exists, both internally and externally. Thus, it is fundamentally important to also focus on the pre-crisis period, the time before a crisis begins (Falkheimer & Heide, 2012). The organizations that are most successful in preventing or surviving crises are those that have adopted crisis awareness as an integral part of their culture. This sort of culture means that risk and possible crisis are constantly on the agenda and employees and managers look out for signs of abnormalities or mistakes. This in turn requires an open and tolerant communication climate and ensuring that the employees themselves are experts in using the necessary resources.

7 Mediatization

From traditional to social media

Strategic communication is often associated with media relations and publicity issues. This can be explained from both a historical and a contemporary perspective. Historically speaking, public relations in the United States developed as a result of the emergence of mass media and the critique of both large companies and national states, as well as of the need for advocacy in connection with war efforts. There are, however, risks associated with seeing the development of public relations in the United States as a global phenomenon, as pointed out by the British researcher Jacquie L'Etang (2004b). The growth of public relations in several European countries cannot be entirely related to the development of mass media, industrialism, or wars. A major factor in these countries was the growing need of public authorities to inform and educate citizens.

Regardless of the reason for the growth of public relations, the mass media and specifically journalists have been key target groups for communication professionals for a long time. For public and political organizations, public relations have for long included constructing creative media strategies that retrospectively defend actions or misdeeds or proactively create visibility for new products, services, ideas, reforms, and so forth. Since the operations of these organizations are funded by public tax money, journalists have a keen interest in scrutinizing them. That said, public and political organizations have their own reasons for actively trying to generate media publicity. As shown in a content analysis conducted by Fredriksson and Pallas (2013), visibility is an important aspect of most public authorities' communication policies.

Debate often surrounds the use of strategic communication by public authorities to build or try to influence public opinion. Critics argue that taxpayer money should not be used for this purpose, while defenders argue that public authorities need to communicate their particular knowledge in order to inform citizens and politicians. There can be a number of reasons for a public media campaign. For example, a campaign may be geared towards affecting the social behavior of citizens through information campaigns, such as encouraging blood donation or the wearing of seatbelts or bicycle helmets. It is also possible that a public authority wishes to try to legitimize their status in relation to decision-makers and ministries. In contrast, corporations, especially those that are operating B2B (business to business), often find it difficult to create media publicity about new products or services. Although there are exceptions, such as popular culture services and products (music, movies, etc.), travel, and cars, for the most part corporations only attract the attention of journalists when there is a crisis or scandal.

There is inevitably conflict between journalists and communication professionals. To put it simply, journalists consider themselves as representatives of the public interest, while communication professionals are seen as tied to special interests. Journalists believe they have higher moral value than communication professionals, regarded as even a bit malign. In the public eye, journalists are usually not to be trusted any more than communication professionals. However, the division between public interest and special interest is valid and should not be dismissed. The role of professional and independent journalism in a democracy is crucial and should be respected.

The growth in the number of communication professionals (on the staff and bought in) since the 1990s has not been matched by an increase in the number of journalists. In 2013 the American Pew Research Institute found there was an approximate 4:1 ratio of communication professionals to journalists in the USA. This ratio is probably also valid, with exceptions, in several other countries where communication professionals have been growing in number and where journalists lost their jobs due to new media uses and structures. This can in large part be credited to the model on which for too long modern media companies have built their businesses, which no longer works in our digitized economy and leads to fewer, more stressed-out journalists working in poorer conditions.

In the past few decades, more and more companies have developed their media relations and directed more resources at these as a part of their marketing mix. PR agencies and sometimes advertising agencies may be hired to generate publicity for both corporate brands and specific products and services. Success was earlier often measured by the frequency of any mention of brand or company name in press clippings or television items. But due to digitalization, increasingly sophisticated computer-based methods for planning and measuring media coverage impact on individuals and groups.

The efforts of communication professionals to position strategic communication as a management function or process rather than support function may have led people to believe that media relations are no longer as important as they were. Furthermore, if one looks at Dozier et al.'s (1995) five models for public relations (see Table 1.1), the media-focused publicity model is both the oldest and the most questionable. However, it is also possible to integrate a late modern way of working with media relations into some of the two-way communication models. In this case, media relations are characterized as a service aimed at journalists, based on a belief that information must always be true and honest if long-term relationships are to be maintained. Media relations, including social media relations, are still at the core of communication professionals' everyday work. According to the 2017 European Communication Monitor, communication professionals think that social media and social networks are the most important channel platforms. Media relations with online newspapers/magazines are also considered crucial, and over half of the respondents still think that media relations with television, radio, and print newspapers are important (Zerfass et al., 2017)

Previously it was relatively common for persons with a journalistic background to become communication professionals. Although this still happens today, it is now much commoner that communication professionals have other backgrounds and are educated in other fields. Strategic communication is only partly geared towards media relations; for the most part, strategic communication is aimed at relations with other stakeholders or groups, such as employees, citizens, customers, investors, local communities, or politicians. Despite this, media relations are still, as already mentioned, an important dimension of strategic communications in both research and practice. This can be explained by the correlation between the expansion of strategic communication in society and the greater importance of mediated communication. For most organizations, increased pressure by investigating journalists is one of the main driving forces behind the creation of communication functions and the use of communications consultants.

In communications research, interest in organizations and their communications strategies towards the media has grown in recent years. There are two directions and platforms for this research. The first platform is media and journalism research, which is often based on the idea that the development of strategic communication affects and threatens independent journalists. Such studies can be connected to Habermas's communication theory (see Chapter 2): media strategies constitute hidden strategic action (Habermas, 1984). The second platform is public relations research that is primarily intended to contribute to more effective media strategies for organizations. The term "news management" has emerged during the past few years, used to describe research that tries to combine media studies and public relations (Falkheimer, 2012).

Special or general interest?

The relationship between journalists and communication professionals has been studied for decades, with a specific focus on how journalists gather information and which sources they use. In contrast to communication professionals, journalists want to work independently of special interest actors. Both communication professionals and journalists are socialized into their roles through education and experience. Power is a central question in this relationship: communication professionals aim to control and advance their interests, whereas journalists are seen as critical investigators. Contextual conditions play a large role for the power relations between communication professionals and journalists; for example, journalists in Sweden are educated and work within the boundaries of ethical press rules, which among other things state that journalists must provide accurate news, check the facts, respect personal integrity, and listen to both parties in a conflict. These principles are common all over the world for professional journalists. Journalism is connected to freedom of speech and in democratic countries considered a societal institution of major importance. Still, laws, rules, and regulations for journalism and media institutions differ all over the world. Communication professionals adhere to various ethical codes, but these tend not to have the same impact due to the fact that their professional identity is not as strong.

The ethical codes of journalists and communication professionals may appear not so distinctly different, and can of course be problematized in both directions. Communication professionals undeniably represent special interests, but they can at the same time argue that their role is to adapt organizations to society's expectations and demands and stakeholders' interests. Journalists consider themselves to be representatives of the public interest who have an important investigative function within democratic systems. However, journalists are also part of media organizations that have their own interests, such as maximizing their reader, watcher, or listener base. For private media companies this is a commercial goal, whereas for public media services this goal serves to meet various political ends.

Since Donald Trump became president of the USA in 2016, the debate around the relationship between journalists and politicians has become increasingly relevant. President Trump and his advisors have criticized journalists and media companies for creating "fake news", lying and being biased. In Great Britain and in many other countries where political leaders and parties have placed a high value on media relations and opinion-making over the last decades, the critique has been reversed – journalists question politicians' PR stunts and the possible role of communication professionals as spin doctors. Interest of this sort peaked during the time when Labour politician and prime minister (1997–2007) Tony Blair held power; Blair, with help from his advisors, adapted much of his politics and work to fit the media logic. The concept of "spin", with its American roots, soon became popular in Britain— used to illustrate how Blair employed a variety of tactics to try to manipulate the media. Spin is often referred to by the media to show how different actors try to influence it by using, for example, biased facts, gambits, and pseudo-events. These negative associations have become dominant in many countries, where there has been hot debate on the role of spin in politics.

We will now highlight a number of theories related to these issues, including previous research on news values, framing, and a development of the agenda-setting theory that was introduced in Chapter 1. We will follow this with a discussion of communication professionals' opportunities and conditions and more applied ideas about organizations' media strategies.

News value

The question of what actually becomes news has long been of interest to researchers. News value can be analyzed from two viewpoints: first, we can assume that certain events in themselves are in and of themselves more or less newsworthy than others (for example, a crime involving celebrities); second, we can see newsworthiness as a construction process, in which certain events are transformed and shaped in order to fulfill specific news criteria.

One of the first and most referenced studies about news value was conducted by the Norwegian researchers Johan Galtung and Mari Holmboe Ruge (1965). These researchers conducted a qualitative content analysis of how international events were presented in the Norwegian press and found a number of common characteristics for the events that ultimately became news. These principles are still valid and are comparable to generic ideas in rhetoric and dramaturgy. An event becomes news if:

- it happens under a short period of time
- it is intense
- it is easy to explain
- it is culturally adjacent
- it is consonant, meaning that it will assimilate cognitively
- it is surprising
- it constitutes a series of clear dramaturgy and
- it is congruent with the community' socio-cultural frame of reference.

Although Galtung and Holmboe Ruge felt that these principles were only common in Western countries, increasing cultural globalization raises the question of whether these principles are now valid for all countries with entrenched democratic media systems. Cultural differences between newsrooms around the world are in all likelihood quite modest, and comparative studies have shown that news about political elites, crime, and sex is priority material in most countries (Manning, 2001).

How the media handle a topic ultimately affects how the media consumers relate to the topic: increased exposure leads to increased interest. This goes without saying for communication professionals who try to create maximum exposure. This supposition can be traced to agenda-setting theory, which was briefly presented in Chapter 2. This communication theory was first proposed by the researchers Maxwell McCombs and Donald Shaw in 1972 and, according to a literature review (Bryant & Miron, 2004), it was the most used theory in three leading scientific communication journals from 1956–2000.

The first study was conducted in Chapel Hill in North Carolina, USA, at the same time as the 1968 presidential campaign. The researchers were interested in finding out how the media affected undecided voters. To simplify the findings: the media had a large effect on which questions were discussed and considered important during the campaign period, but they did not necessarily affect the outcome of these discussions. This is considered the first level of media agenda-setting power. In the forty years since this initial research, at least four hundred additional studies on agenda-setting power have been undertaken (McCombs & Shaw, 1972) and interest has moved to the second level. Starting with the idea that the media decide how topics on the agenda are prioritized, the question moves to whether the media also effect how individuals draw conclusions and make decisions.

One direction of agenda-setting theory is especially interested in media portrayals, the framing of issues and events, and the impact that frames have on media consumers (Iyengar, 1991; Semetko & Valkenburg, 2000). Research has shown that it significant that the media tend to present politics as a "game of scandals" rather than a matter of ideology or substantive debate (Strömbäck, 2000). Some argue that the media's focus on scandals and political games as part of a strategic negative campaigning exercise (planting negative news about the opposing party or candidate) actually increases general interest in politics. However, the question arises whether this increased interest could actually have a dark side: an extended gap of trust that in the long term threatens the very foundation of democracy – participation in elections.

Media framing is based on four properties (Entman, 1993):

- the media define the problems
- the media depict the causation
- the media express moral values and
- the media indicate possible solutions.

The theory of framing, with its background in social psychology (Goffman, 1959), has been widely used in media and communication research and shows that the media do not only set the agenda. According to one study on media and political communication, news media outlets use five different frames when they report events (Semetko & Valkenburg, 2000). The first frame is an accountability frame, through which the media ask, who is responsible? This is a typical frame in crises, when the reporting usually begins with the event and then moves to questions of accountability. The second frame is a conflict frame, in which the media suggest conflict between different actors. This occurs in most news. The third is a moral frame, through which the media analyze to what extent the event violates moral norms. Different cultural contexts have different moral standards. One example of this can be seen in the major media exposure in Sweden of student harassment and mistreatment at the private boarding school Lundsberg in August 2013, which ultimately caused the school to temporarily close. A school such as Lundsberg, which in Sweden (with its strong views regarding equality) is associated with the upper class, is an anomaly that in itself goes against cultural and moral norms. Thus, when a scandal of this sort occurs, media interest is much greater than it would be for a public (i.e. state) school.

The fourth frame is financial: the media can focus their reporting on, for example, the economic consequences of an event. Finally, the media can give their reporting a human-interest perspective and show the consequences of an event for private individuals.

Of course, it is not only the media that create frames: many parties in practice endeavor to frame issues. Communication professionals, for example, try to establish frames that they consider correct or legitimate. Politicians and business leaders refer to the established ideological framework, rooted in cultural norms, and through this framework communicate simple messages adapted to public opinion. The public may have both common and differing frameworks for understanding and interpreting a social event, but it is also affected by the news media frames. Furthermore, the emergence of social media has increased the number of possible frames, the result being various simultaneous media frames.

Sources and journalists

The great dispute within news management is whether it is communication professionals or journalists who have most power over media content. News sources can be defined in many ways. The definition that we use, and that we have taken from Cameron, Sallot and Curtin (1997), is simple: a news source is a person or organization that through some channel conveys information to a journalist or media organization. Of special interest within strategic communication are the sources that the Norwegian media researcher Sigurd Allern calls "professional source organizations" (Allern, 1997); that is to say, the established major actors in society that either have or use specialist communicative competence.

The first independent model is a sort of ideal state of affairs from a journalistic perspective. It is common that journalists consider this to be what is true in practice. Few journalists admit that professional sources, media strategies, and actors influence them and their production. However, there are many studies that demonstrate how professional sources influence the media. In a classic study, media researcher Herbert Gans (1979) concluded:

> The relationship between sources and journalists resembles a dance, for sources seek access to journalists, and journalists seek access to sources. Although it takes two to tango, either sources or journalists can lead, but more often than not, sources do the leading.
>
> (p. 116)

Researcher Stuart Hall conducted one of the key studies in this field in the 1970s. This work gave the official sources the title "primary definers" (Hall, 1978). In this study, it was the police and other public authorities that formulated problems, steered the news agenda, and were used as credible sources by the media. The primary definers' reliability was determined by three factors: they were already powerful, they were considered to have a legitimate representative function, and some of them, such as objective scientists, had expert status.

The British researcher Paul Manning (2001) argued in a later analysis that it is the pressure to meet deadlines and produce newsworthy content that lies behind the use of primary definers. These sources are newsworthy because they affect the lives of individuals. This means that the media prioritize actors with power and marginalizes other groups and institutions; the power structure is reproduced through the news process. The same need lies behind media reliance on news agencies and other media or journalists as sources. The media is trying to rationalize and minimize costs: this becomes especially clear when it comes to fields that fall outside the media's own core business, when other media and news agencies dominate as sources.

The development of media and communication has undoubtedly led to greater interdependence between sources and journalists. The changing conditions of journalism and the digitalization and professionalization of strategic communication challenges traditional journalism. Due to faster speed of information, increased production requirements, and new forms of media and market logics, journalists are increasingly dependent on their sources. Sponsorship of TV programmes and the development of online newspapers with integrated content marketing are examples of trends that demonstrate how the traditional borders between journalists, public relations, and marketing are being challenged. Convergence between previously separate roles, technologies, and media content is one of the strongest trends in our communications landscape (Jenkins, 2006).

Strategies for sources

Each source has its own qualifications and needs to adapt itself to the news and media outlets' varying structural demands. Generally speaking, the highest news value comes from events with short cultural and geographical distance in relation to the target groups of the media; this is relatively obvious. There are several reasons why a source might be of interest to journalists:

- *Previous contact and suitability.* If a source is already established as reputable then it has more chance to influence journalists. Sources that are good at communicating clear, short messages and fit into the pre-made dramaturgy of a news story are often used by journalists. If a source has expert status and is considered independent (e.g. by association with a university or another media company), the interest increases. The value of having previously used journalist contacts is one explanation for why PR agencies are often employed to handle media relations. Here there is a substantial distance between theory and practice. Research in media studies and strategic communication rarely deals with relationships at the inter-personal micro level. Instead, researchers take a macro-level perspective, looking at the relationships between organizations and institutional interests or actors. However, in practice it is the interpersonal, local, and direct relationships that are of greatest significance.
- *Productivity.* This concerns the capacity of the source to give journalists newsworthy and relevant information. Distributing a large amount of

press material to editors, when only a small proportion of the information has news value, does not go down well. This can be a serious problem for journalists, who are bombarded by different sources with email, press kits, and phone calls. The capacity to understand what is newsworthy is not the key to success – that assessment should be made before the information is conveyed. The management of many organizations lack a proper understanding of what events are given space by the media; it is therefore important that the communication professionals act critically and represent viewpoints appropriate to the surrounding environment.

- *Reliability.* Sources who provide trivial or dubious information lose their authority. This is of course clearly connected to the two previous criteria. Though it is not impossible to make such information appear newsworthy or serious, if it comes to light that the information was unreliable and was reported on false grounds, the reporter will dismiss future messages from the source as unreliable.
- *Authority.* Public actors or those with established authority in a field, such as government representatives or researchers, have an advantage. However, it is important not to manipulate without reason the story or message through connections to authorities; this only affects reliability and long-term relationships.
- *Eloquence.* In interviews, the source must be articulate and adapt information to the journalist's need for simplicity, clarity, and dramatization. This is incredibly important and means that communication professionals must educate all potential spokespersons in their organization. Some organizations strategically select only one or two executives as spokespersons, but this strategy can go wrong. There is a risk that all other potential spokespersons within the organization refer all questions to these individuals, making journalists suspect that something is wrong. Ideally, as many people as possible in an organization should be trained in how to effectively express themselves.

Researchers Scott M. Cutlip, Allen H. Center, and Glenn M. Broom (2006) give some concrete advice to prospective sources. Among other things, they stress that a source should begin by expressing the societal aspect of a topic and not (at least not specifically) the interests of the organization, as "advertising" statements strongly conflict with journalistic independence and review requirements. This can often be a problem when professional marketers and salespeople communicate with journalists. It is also important that the source defines what is and is not applicable to a topic, rather than repeating the (often leading) questions that journalists pose. In tactical terms, there are many ways to consider this. For example, a news source should never speculate about the reasons for an event, should not be fooled by "counterpart" statements provided by the journalist ("But I spoke to Mr. X who said that …"), and should avoid obscuring relevant information. A professional source defines their answers and has the ability to redefine journalists' questions when

necessary. Researcher Richard Bailey (2006), who has long practical experience, has formulated four golden rules for good media relations that we also
consider to be ethically defensible:

- Act as a service function for journalists: answer questions quickly and
  objectively, be available, and convey relevant information.
- Respect and accept the independent role of the media (and realize that as
  a source, your role is different).
- Be honest with who you are and what you represent. Never try to cover
  anything up.
- Be just as readily available when the news is bad as when the news is good.

Part III
Future developments

8 Reflections and the communicative organization

In this book, based on research on organizations' targeted communication, our aim has been to provide an overview and discussion of the key theories and practices within the field of strategic communication. There are two sub-fields that we have deliberately not addressed: direct relationships between organizations and capital investors (i.e. investor relations) and between organizations and political decision-makers (i.e. public affairs and lobbying). Both these fields are relatively specialized in practice and do not necessarily place communication issues at the center. In addition, they require very particular knowledge bases, especially in economics, political science or law, and there is no room for such deep diving here. However, we have discussed political communication in its broader sense. For a further investigation of this field, we recommend the book *Political Public Relations* by Strömbäck and Kiousis (2011).

Strategic communication, as we previously emphasized, represents both a knowledge field and a knowledge-based interest. As a field of knowledge it is directly related to the social, economic, cultural and technological developments in our environment, where the borders are constantly moving. We have chosen to emphasize in particular the reflexive and ritual communication perspective, which we believe is of central importance for the field of knowledge and development of practice. This book offers no universal solutions to the various organizational problems. This is because there can be no general solution applicable to all communication problems. Organizational researchers such as Karl E. Weick (2015) actually advises against practitioners spending time, energy, and money trying to find absolute answers or reasons. Our world is so complex and so difficult to predict that a search for *the* solution will not result in much. The world is ambiguous and simple, clear answers are simply not available. Weick emphasizes that in an ambiguous world, the "wrong" rating cannot exist: things are only reasonable or unreasonable and there are always different ways to interpret something. In this book we want to show that solutions to organizational problems depend on situations, contexts, and organizational conditions and that there is always more than one interpretation and thus multiple solutions. At the same time, this does not mean that "anything goes". There are several theories and resources for communication that are timeless, especially with regard to social psychological,

psychological, and rhetorical mechanisms (some of them described in chapter 1). In addition, there is often a right and a wrong way to manage communication problems—but the right and wrong depend on local and specific circumstances. The ability to understand what is going on between different stakeholders and an organization is crucial for making good decisions.

Today, there is no general agreement regarding what value and meaning strategic communication has for organizations and society. There are tentative ideas and specific results from empirical studies, but there is still a massive need for more knowledge. One of the main issues, debated in research as well as practice, is why organizations should even make use communication professionals. As mentioned in Chapter 3, the value of strategic practice (focusing the effect on the overall goals and missions of an organization or on society) is hard to measure, while it is easier to measure the effects on a tactical and organization-centric level—for example, the results of a communication campaign in attitude or behavior change among stakeholders.

Within marketing communication it has long been possible to show the effects of communication activities such as marketing campaigns. This can be explained quite simply: the marketing of products and services is directly related to sales. In scientific terms it is of course not that easy to find and show simple links between an advertising campaign and sales. There are a variety of factors (or variables) that interact, and contexts and situations vary. No advertising agency has patented a simple, universal formula for effective advertising. However, some measurement methods have been developed for finding relationships. For those involved in strategic communication, it has always been a problem to demonstrate clear effects. This is partly due to the complex nature of the communication, but also because there are few major empirical studies looking for strategic communication effects. Nevertheless, practitioners have grown in number and more and more organizations are focusing on strategic communication in different forms. We have designed a model (see Figure 8.1 below) that summarizes and links the most common arguments behind strategic communication initiatives—where strategic

Figure 8.1 The goals of strategic communication

communication is supposed to create value. The model illustrates the four main goals of strategic communication and may be used for further studies.

A few important points have to be made regarding the goals model. First, strategic communication efforts can be motivated by the fact that they are believed to contribute to the organization's effectiveness. For example, knowledge will be applied that encourages employees to use the right channels for the correct message in the "correct way". In practice, managers can be educated in how they should communicate with different stakeholders for best results and how internal and external channels should be organized to make the communication flow more time and resource efficient and improve employee information (target group customization) or planning and training in crisis communication. However, it is difficult to demonstrate measurable results of such activity, even if you assume that strategic communication in qualitative terms has positive effects.

Second, communication efforts can be seen as important for the creation, maintenance or enhancement of the organization's image, defined here as the superficial knowledge that people around the organization have about the organization. There is a clear relation here to advertising and trademarks, especially in the case of corporate branding (organization brands). Organization brands, of course, are the focus of communication professionals, especially with regard to legitimacy and trust: strategic communication is supposed to adapt organizations' activities and behavior to internal and external circumstances and needs, with the overriding goal of creating long-term legitimacy. Sometimes the work with organizational image deals with the production and distribution of media-related information (press releases, press conferences, digital presence, opinion polls, event arrangements, etc.). A general assumption, even if it is now challenged by the development of digital platforms, is that the journalistic coverage is of great importance for organizations, especially in the context of crises or scandals. There is also an arsenal of measurement methods to use, as well as a long tradition of media research. It is not really possible to discern any general relationships, but one may demonstrate individual relationships between the media image and trust, attitudes, and behaviors.

Third, strategic communication is motivated by its assumed contribution to changing or strengthening the organization's identity for its employees and thereby the organizational culture. There is a clear link to organizational efficiency, but it mainly concerns valuation and cultural aspects. Good communication is believed to lead to a positive community around the value base of an organization, which in turn supports the organization's vision and strategy—"everyone going in the same direction". The tools used to support organizational efficiency and image can also be considered important for this mission. For example, publicity in the media may be of greater significance for coworkers than for external stakeholders. However, it is difficult to show measurable and causal relationships between communication efforts and organizational identity. This is because "culture" and "identity" are extremely qualitative concepts and relate more to interpretation than effects.

Fourth and last, strategic communication can be justified on the basis that it promotes transparency between the organization's members and between the organization, the stakeholders, and the external environment. This argument is normative and based on a non-authoritarian and democratic view of organizations and society, meaning that closure, hierarchy, and information retention are negatively assessed. This is not, of course, an organizational efficiency perspective, though so often claimed, especially in the context of crisis management. However, it needs to be said that excessive transparency can have negative consequences (for example, uncertainty or inefficiency). In other words, from an efficiency perspective there is no given starting point because it is a normative (value) question. But of course there are opportunities to study the effects, as James Grunig and his colleagues did in part in their Excellent studies.

Communication trends

As mentioned before, strategic communication may be viewed as a product of late modernity. This means that societal trends are of core importance for the future of this field of knowledge. Communication—the creation of shared meaning—will certainly never lose its importance for any society or organization. But times change and the need for both basic and applied theories and methods for communication aimed at achieving overall organizational goals will not decrease. According to the European Communication Monitor (an annual survey directed at communication professionals in 42 European countries), the main challenge is to link business strategy and communication. Communication professionals themselves have a strong belief in the value of strategic communication for organizational success, but top management in organizations still tend to view communication mainly as a support function, not a managerial process of core relevance (Brønn, 2014; Falkheimer et al., 2017). Among other challenges for the future are the role of visual communication, which professionals find increasingly important but lack operational knowledge about, and coping with the digital evolution, which demands lifelong learning to remain up to date in (Zerfass, Tench, Verčič, Verhoeven, & Moreno, 2017).

The macro trends of late modernity will not disappear but rather become deeper due to social, technological, political, and economic development. They all have consequences for strategic communication. One basic macro trend is increasing *perceived uncertainty* among human beings regarding their different roles as citizens, consumers, and so forth. Access to information about basically everything increases globally due to digitalization. This development is, from a democratic approach, pretty amazing. Today we can build social networks and gather information in ways that were impossible only some decades ago. But increased access to information also leads to more choices for human beings. Making a choice means taking risks, which in turn leads to uncertainty. Strategic communication is relevant in this context since organizations need to make themselves legitimate through communication to be "chosen" by customers, citizens, members, and so forth. In other words, increased uncertainty leads to an increased need of strategic communication by organizations. Another basic macro trend is *individualization,* a modern movement with its roots in the Enlightenment of the eighteenth century. The mass communication theories of the last century have slowly been replaced with theories about communication that do not rely on an image of humans as masses or target groups. The active stakeholder and political consumer are typical individualistic roles that have effects on the organizations of today. Increasingly, people expect and demand individual and personalized communication from organizations. New media technologies have created possibilities for adapting information to the individual, based on information that may be collected through our digital footprints. This evolution is positive in some ways but may also threaten our integrity, since information about us as individuals may be used for control and surveillance. From a strategic communication standpoint the opportunities to learn more about stakeholders are huge, but so are the ethical problems. A third basic macro trend is *mobility,* a concept that can be understood in several ways. One very simple example is physical mobility, the fact that late modern humans travel more and more easily than before. But mobility may also be interpreted as a social phenomenon: peoples' attitudes and behavior is in constant flux, they are not constant or easy to define with simple market surveys but can change as a result of actions and things that happen. The role of strategic communication is relevant here in many ways. One example is how we consume information today. The launch of iPphone 2007 has had a major impact on access to and speed of information, making it both easier and more problematic to work with strategic communication. The traditional gatekeeping role of journalists, editors, and the like has changed and rumors as well as accurate information travel faster and further in a profoundly new way. A tweet from current US president Trump is visible and spread in seconds: as soon as he presses *send* the whole world can read his latest opinion.

From an organizational perspective, there are several trends that emerge in strategic communication. We have touched upon most of them in this book, but let us recall the most significant. First, the strict separation of so-called internal and external communication is being challenged. To reach overall organizational goals, communication professionals must integrate the internal and external communication processes. Organizations are not closed rooms and coworkers must be viewed as partners in strategic communication on a broad scale. Second, the integration of traditional goal-oriented communication disciplines such as marketing communication, advertising, organizational communication, and public relations will continue. By using an outside-in approach, communications may be organized and executed in a processual rather than unidirectional fashion. Finally, digitalization—as mentioned above—makes new demands on strategic communication as a professional field. The digitalization of media landscapes challenges the transmission communication approach and opens up new roles for communication professionals and new opportunities to interact with stakeholders. At the same time, digitalization enables new forms of unethical communication and propaganda.

Forward-looking reflections

The future of strategic communication as a practice and field of knowledge is bright. An increasing number of researchers are interested in the issues we deal with in this book. More and better-trained professionals further develop their skills in different ways. At the risk of simplifying the historical development, we want to highlight three trends that we consider of crucial importance for the future of the field.

First, we want to highlight the importance of embracing a meaningful and reflexive approach to strategic communication. Traditional efforts to create general communication models and explain direct and causal relationships through quantitative and statistical research are valuable, but they should increasingly be joined by close-up observations of organizations' strategic communication. To answer some of the questions, researchers need to act more as anthropologists than as scientists.

Second, it is important to embrace a critical perspective on strategic communication. Communication may be about participatory engagement, but it is also about power and dominance (Heide, 2014). In traditional research, power issues have often been neglected in favor of applied studies. But critical research can also contribute to increased reflection and to professionalization (Falkheimer & Heide, 2016). The fact that ethical issues have been high on practitioners' agendas for several years is a clear sign of greater self-awareness. There is no doubt that strategic communication is also about power and ethical choices. As mentioned before, strategic communication is a double-edged sword that may be used for good or bad. Criticism and self-criticism is necessary for professional development. Although the future looks bright for strategic communication as an organizational practice in the sense that it increases its importance, the consequences of this should be highlighted critically, in particular from a democratic point of view. The same applies to the manipulative use of the tactics that strategic communication involves; as with rhetoric, tactics can be used for both good and evil, depending on values.

Third, it is important to realize the importance of improvisation (cf. Cunha, Clegg, Rego, & Neves, 2014; Falkheimer & Heide, 2010). A point of departure that has been consistent in this book is that strategic communication based on rigid plans, where it is assumed that organizations can control and predict the future, is impossible to implement. We have stressed that a reflexive approach is required—that is, thinking about how one's own starting points and how actions influence the outcome (Falkheimer & Heide, 2016). This means that if our original plans are too tight, we become less flexible and innovative and risk not being able to act fast enough. It is important to have a clear strategic framework (Falkheimer et al., 2017). But only those who have developed the ability to improvise within this framework can become a master of strategic communication. From a knowledge perspective, this means there is a need to be open to ideas and methods emanating from the creative field (e.g. music, theatre, film, dance).

The communicative organization

A fundamental idea of this book is that communication constitutes organizations (CCO—which is conveniently also an acronym for chief communications officer or, sometimes, corporate communications officer). CCO consists of "a collection of perspectives about grounding the role of communication in the ontology of organizations" (Putnam & Nicotera, 2010, p. 158). Communication is thus not only a variable that can be controlled and managed, but the very means by which an organization exists. Some researchers, such as Weick (1995), see communication as a synonym for organization. Without communication, organizations would cease to exist. CCO researchers (e.g. Cooren et al., 2011) claim that it is more proper to talk about organizing processes for which communication is a prerequisite. Organization is in other words perceived as a verb or *process* of becoming. This reasoning is fundamental to the communicative organization that was introduced in the academic world a couple of years ago (Heide & Simonsson, 2014). There is no common definition of the communicative organization, but the assumption is that organizations that communicate well with important stakeholders have a competitive advantage. The communicative organization also embraces "an overall knowledge and awareness of the importance of communication for continuous organizing processes that enact and reproduce an organization" (Falkheimer et al., 2017, p. 93 f).

The communicative organization is also a concept that gained increasing popularity among practitioners. The communicative organization was launched in 2010 by the 6th World Public Relations Forum—The Stockholm Accords (Global Alliance, 2010). This report emphasized that chief communication officers cannot manage or control more than 10 percent of an organization's communication. Consequently, in the communicative organization there is a broad understanding that all organizational members—managers and employees—are *strategic communicators*. As a consequence of this, chief communication officers have two strategic roles:

- A *political role*—providing management with all the necessary current information to enable it to both effectively lead the value networks and make a conscious, intelligent, and enduring attempt to understand the relevant dynamics of society at large.
- A *contextual role* that involves the continuous provision of communicative skills, competencies, and tools for members of the host networks so that they can improve the quality of their relationships, thereby creating greater organizational value.

We firmly believe that the communicative organization is a useful concept that communication professionals can employ to talk about the value of communication. To talk about and set the goal of becoming a communicative organization is a way to put communication on the organizational agenda, to highlight the importance of communication, to embrace the complexity of communication, and to realize that all organizational members are ambassadors of the organization. In all internal and external interactions, the organization—the brand, the reputation, and the identity—is produced and reproduced.

References

Åberg, L. (1990). Theoretical model and praxis of total communication. *International public relations review*, 13(2), 13–16.

Ackoff, R. L. (1970). *A concept of corporate planning*. New York: Wiley-Interscience.

Adorno, T., & Horkneimer, M. (1944). *Dialectic of enlightment*. New York: Continuum.

Allern, S. (1997). *Når kildene byr opp til dans: En sökelys på profesjonelle kildeorganisasjoners mediestrategier og nyhetsinnflytelse*. Bergen: Universitetet i Bergen, Institutt for Journalistikk.

Altheide, D. L. (2004). Media logic and political communication. *Political Communication*, 21(3), 293–296.

Altheide, D. L., & Snow, R. P. (1979). *Media logic*. Beverly Hills, CA: Sage.

Alvesson, M. (2003). Beyond neopositivists, romantics, and localists: A reflexive approach to interviews in organizational research. *Academy of Management Review*, 28 (1), 13–33.

Alvesson, M. (2011). *Interpreting interviews*. London: Sage.

Alvesson, M. (2013). *The triumph of emptiness: Consumption, higher education, and work organization*. Oxford: Oxford University Press.

Alvesson, M., & Kärreman, D. (2000a). Taking the linguistic turn in organizational research: Challenges, responses, consequences. *Journal of Applied Behavioral Science*, 36(2), 136–158.

Alvesson, M., & Kärreman, D. (2000b). Varieties of discourse: On the study of organizations through discourse analysis. *Human Relations*, 53(9), 11–25.

Alvesson, M., & Kärreman, D. (2011a). Decolonializing discourse: Critical reflections on organizational discourse analysis. *Human Relations*, 64(9), 1121–1146.

Alvesson, M., & Kärreman, D. (2011b). *Qualitative research and theory development: Mystery as method*. London: Sage.

Alvesson, M., & Kärreman, D. (2013). The closing of critique, pluralism and reflexivity: A response to hardy and grant and some wider reflections. *Human Relations*, 66(10), 1353–1371.

Alvesson, M., & Spicer, A. (2012). A stupidity-based theory of organizations. *Journal of Management Studies*, 49(7), 1194–1220.

Alvesson, M., & Sveningsson, S. (2016). *Changing organizational culture: Cultural change work in progress* (2nd ed.). Abingdon: Routledge.

Ansoff, H. I. (1965). *Corporate strategy: An analytic approach to business policy for growth and expansion*. New York: McGraw-Hill.

Aristotle. (1959). *Ars rhetorica*. Oxford: Oxford University Press.

Arpan, L. M., & Roskos-Ewoldsen, D. R. (2005). Stealing thunder: Analysis of the effects of proactive disclosure of crisis information. *Public Relations Review*, 31(3), 425–433.

Ashby, W. R. (1956). *An introduction to cybernetics*. London: Chapman & Hall.

Axley, S. R. (1984). Managerial and organizational communication in terms of the conduit metaphor. *Academy of Management Review*, 9(3), 428–437.

Bailey, R. (2006). Media relations. In R. Tench & L. Yeomans (Eds.), *Exploring public relations* (pp. 318). Harlow,: FT Prentice Hall.

Barker, R. (2013). Strategic integrated communication: An alternative perspective of integrated marketing communication? *Communicatio*, 39(1), 102–121.

Barker, R., & Angelopulo, G. C. (2013). *Integrated organisational communication* (3rd ed.). Cape Town: Juta.

Barnard, C. I. (1938/1968). *The functions of the executive*. Cambridge, MA: Harvard University Press.

Barney, J. (2002). Strategic management: From informed conversation to academic discipline. *Academy of Management Executive*, 16(2), 53–57.

Barratt-Pugh, L., Bahn, S., & Gakere, E. (2013). Managers as change agents: Implications for human resource managers engaging with culture change. *Journal of Change Management*, 26(4), 748–764.

Baudrillard, J. (1994). *Simulacra and simulations*. Ann Arbor, MI: University of Michigan Press.

Bauman, Z. (2000). *Liquid modernity*. Cambridge: Polity Press.

Bauman, Z., & May, T. (2001). *Thinking sociologically*. Malden, MA: Blackwell.

Beck, U. (1992). *Risk society: Towards a new modernity*. London: Sage.

Beer, M., & Nohria, N. (Eds.). (2000). *Breaking the code of change*. Boston, MA: Harvard Business School Press.

Bell, S. H., & Bell, E. C. (1976). Public relations: Functional or functionary? *Public Relations Review*, 2(3), 47–57.

Benoit, W. L. (1995). *Accounts, excuses, and apologies: A theory of image restoration strategies*. Albany, NY: State University of New York Press.

Benoit, W. L. (2004). Image repair discourse and crisis communication. In D. P. Millar & R. L. Heath (Eds), *Responding to crisis: A rhetorical approach to crisis communication* (pp. 263–280). Mahwah, NJ: Lawrence Erlbaum.

Benoit, W. L. (2013). Image repair strategy. In R. L. Heath (Ed.), *Encyclopedia of public relations*. Thousand Oaks, CA: Sage.

Bernays, E. L. (1955). *The engineering of consent*. Norman: University of Oklahoma Press

Bies, R. J., & Shapiro, D. L. (1988). Voice and justification: Their influence on procedural fairness judgements. *Academy of Management Journal*, 31(3), 676–686.

Bland, M. (1998). *Communicating out of a crisis*. Basingstoke: Macmillan.

Boorstin, D. (1963/1985). *The image: A guide to pseudo-events in America*. New York: Atheneum.

Botan, C. H., & Taylor, M. (2004). Public relations: State of the field. *Journal of Communication*, 54(4), 645–661.

Bowen, S. A. (2009). What communication professionals tell us regarding dominant coalition access and gaining membership. *Journal of Applied Communication Research*, 37(4), 418–443.

Broms, H., & Gahmberg, H. (1983). Communication to self in organizations and cultures. *Administrative Science Quarterly*, 28(3), 482–495.

Brønn, P. S. (2014). How others see us: Leaders' perceptions of communication and communication managers. *Journal of Communication Management*, 18(1), 58–79.

Broom, G. M. (1982). A comparison of sex roles in public relations. *Public Relations Review*, 8(3), 17–22.

Broom, G. M., & Dozier, D. M. (1986). Advancement for public relations role models. *Public Relations Review*, 12(1), 37–56.

Broom, G. M., & Smith, G. D. (1979). Testing the practitioner's impact on clients. *Public Relations Review*, 5(3), 47–59. Bryant, J., & Miron, D. (2004). Theory and research in mass communication. *Journal of Communication*, 54(4), 662–704. Burke, W. W. (2011). A perspective on the field of organization development and change: The zeigarnik effect. *Journal of Applied Behavioral Science*, 47(2), 143–167.

Burris, E. R. (2012). The risks and rewards of speaking up: Managerial responses to employee voice. *Academy of management journal*, 55(4), 851–875.

Cameron, G., Sallot, L., & Curtin, P. (1997). Public relations and the production of news. A critical review and theoretical framework. In B. R. Burleson (Ed.), *Communication yearbook 20* (pp. 111–155). Thousand Oaks, CA: Sage.

Carey, J. (2009). *Communication as culture: Essays on media and society*. New York: Routledge.

Carlzon, J. (1989). *Moments of truth*. New York: Perennial Library.

Chaffee, E. E. (1985). Three models of strategy. *Academy of Management Review*, 10(1), 89–98.

Chandler, A. D. (1962). *Strategy and structure: Chapters in the history of the industrial enterprise*. New York: Anchor Books.

Cheney, G., & Christensen, L. T. (2001a). Organizational identity: Linkages between internal and external communication. In F. M. Jablin & L. L. Putnam (Eds), *Organizational communication: Advances in theory, research, and methods*. Thousand Oaks, CA: Sage.

Cheney, G., & Christensen, L. T. (2001b). Public relations as contested terrain: A critical response. In R. L. Heath (Ed.), *Handbook of public relations*. Thousand Oaks, CA: Sage.

Cheney, G., & Christensen, L. T. (2006). What should public relations theory do, practically speaking? *Journal of Communication Management*, 10(1), 100–102.

Cheney, G., Christensen, L. T., Zorn, T. E., & Ganesh, S. (Eds). (2011). *Organizational communication in an age of globalization: Issues, reflections, practices* (2nd edn). Long Grove, IL: Waveland Press.

Cheney, G., Christensen, L. T., & Dailey, S. (2014). Communicating identity and identification in and around organizations. In L. L. Putnam & D. K. Mumby (Eds), *The Sage handbook of organizational communication: Advances in theory, research, and methods* (pp. 695–716). Thousand Oaks, CA: Sage.

Chia, R. (1995). From modern to postmodern organizational analysis. *Organization Studies*, 16(4), 579–604.

Chia, R. (1996). The problem of reflexitivity in organizational research: Towards a postmodern science of organization. *Organization*, 3(1), 31–59.

Choi, J., & Choi, Y. (2009). Behavioral dimensions of public relations leadership in organizations. *Journal of Communication Management*, 13(4), 292–309.

Christensen, L. T. (2002). Corporate communication: The challenge of transparency. *Corporate Communications: An International Journal*, 7(3), 162–168.

Christensen, L. T., & Cheney, G. (2000). Self-absorption and self-seduction in the corporate identity game. In M. Schultz, M. J. Hatch & M. H. Larsen (Eds), *The expressive organization: Linking identity, reputation, and the corporate brand* (pp. 246–270). Oxford: Oxford University Press.

Christensen, L. T., & Cornelissen, J. (2011). Bridging corporate and organizational communication: Review, development and a look to the future. *Management Communication Quarterly*, 25(3), 383–414.

Christensen, L. T., Firat, A. F., & Cornelissen, J. (2009). New tensions and challenges in integrated communications. *Corporate Communications: An International Journal*, 14(2), 207–219.

Christensen, L. T., Torp, S., & Firat, A. F. (2005). Integrated marketing communication and postmodernity: An odd couple? *Corporate Communications: An International Journal*, 10(2), 156–167.

Clampitt, P. G., DeKoch, R. J., & Cashman, T. (2000). A strategy for communicating about uncertainty. *Academy of Management Executive*, 14(4), 41–58.

Clifton, J. (2015). Leaders as ventriloquists. Leader identity and influencing the communicative construction of the organisation. *Leadership*, 13(3), 301–319.

Coch, L., & French, J. R. P. (1948). Overcoming resistance to change. *Human Relations*, 1(4), 512–532.

Cohen, L., Musson, G., & Tietze, S. (2005). Teaching communication to business and management students. *Management Communication Quarterly*, 19(2), 279–287.

Connolly-Ahern, C. (2008). Strategic communication. In L. L. Kaid & C. Holtz-Bacha (Eds.), *Encyclopedia of political communication* (pp. 765–766). Thousand Oaks, CA: Sage.

Coombs, W. T. (2006). Crisis management: A communicative approach. In C. H. Botan & V. Hazleton (Eds.), *Public relations theory II* (pp. 171–197). Mahwah, NJ: Lawrence Erlbaum.

Coombs, W. T. (2015). *Ongoing crisis communication: Planning, managing, and responding*. Thousand Oaks, CA: Sage.

Coombs, W. T., & Holladay, S. (2007). *It's not just PR: Public relations in society*. Malden, MA: Blackwell Publishing.

Cooren, F., Kuhn, T., & Cornelissen, J. P. (2011). Communication, organizing and organization: An overview and introduction to the special issue. *Organization Studies*, 32(9), 1149–1170.

Cornelissen, J. P. (2000). Theoretical concept or management fashion? Examining the significance of IMC. *Journal of Advertising Research*, 40(5), 1–16.

Cornelissen, J. P. (2011). *Corporate communication: A guide to theory and practice*. London: Sage.

Creedon, P. J. (1991). Public relations and women's work: Toward a feminist analysis of public relations roles. In L. A. Grunig & J. E. Grunig (Eds), *Public relations research annual* (vol. 3, pp. 37–43). Hillsdale, NJ: Lawrence Erlbaum.

Cropp, F., & Pincus, D. J. (2001). The mystery of public relations: Unraveling its past, unmasking its future. In R. L. Heath (Ed.), *Handbook of public relations* (pp. 189–203). Thousand Oaks, CA: Sage.

Cunha, M. P., Clegg, S., Rego, A., & Neves, P. (2014). Organizational improvisation: From the constraint of strict tempo to the power of the avant-garde. *Creativity And Innovation Management*, 23(4), 359–373.

Cutlip, S. M., Center, A. H., & Broom, G. M. (2006). *Effective public relations* (8th ed.). Upper Saddle River, NJ: Prentice Hall.

Cyert, R. M., & March, J. G. (1963). *A behavioral theory of the firm*. Englewood Cliffs, NJ: Prentice Hall.

Czarniawska, B. (2008). *A theory of organizing*. Cheltenham, Glos.: Edward Elgar.

Dahlén, M., Lange, F., & Smith, T. (2010). *Marketing communications: A brand narrative approach*. Chichester: Wiley.

DeBono, E. (1992). *Sur/petition: Going beyond monopolies*. London: Fontana.

Deetz, S. A. (2000). The a priori of the communication community and the hope for solving real problems. In S. Corman & M. S. Poole (Eds.), *Perspectives on organizational communication: Finding the common ground* (pp. 105–112). New York: Guilford.

Deetz, S. A. (2001). Conceptual foundations. In F. M. Jablin & L. L. Putnam (Eds), *The new handbook of organizational communication: Advances in theory, research, and methods* (pp. 3–46). Thousand Oaks, CA: Sage.

Detert, J. R., & Edmondson, A. C. (2011). Implicit voice theories: Taken-for-granted rules of self-censorship at work. *Academy of Management Journal*, 54(3), 461–488.

Dozier, D. M. (1992). The organizational role of communicators and public relations practitioners. In J. E. Grunig (Ed.), *Excellence in public relations and communications management* (pp. 327–356). Hillsdale, NJ: Lawrence Erlbaum.

Dozier, D. M., & Broom, G. M. (1995). Evolution of the managerial role in public relations practive. *Journal of public relations research*, 7(1), 3–26.

Dozier, D. M., Grunig, L. A., & Grunig, J. E. (1995). *Managers's guide to excellence in public relations and communication management*. Mahwah, NJ: Lawrence Erlbaum.

Drucker, P. F. (1955). *The practice of management*. London: Heinemann.

Ellis, N., Fitchett, J., Higgins, M., Jack, G., Lim, M., Saren, M., and Tadejewski, M. (2011). *Marketing: A critical textbook*. London: Sage.

Entman, R. M. (1993). Framing: Toward clarification of a fractured paradigm. *Journal of Communication*, 43(4), 51–58.

Ewen, S. (1996). *PR! The social history of spin*. New York: Basic Books.

Falkheimer, J. (2012). Medierna och kampen om innehållet. In L. Nord & J. Strömbäck (Eds), *Medierna och demokratin*. Lund: Studentlitteratur.

Falkheimer, J. (2016). Digital media and new terrorism. In T. W. Coombs, J. Falkheimer, M. Heide, & P. Young (Eds), *Strategic communication, social media and democracy: The challenge of the digital naturals* (pp. 143–152). London: Routledge.

Falkheimer, J., & Heide, M. (2003). *Reflexiv kommunikation: Nya tankar för strategiska kommunikatörer* ([Reflexive communication: New thoughts for strategic communicators]). Malmö: Liber.

Falkheimer, J., & Heide, M. (2006). Multicultural crisis communication: Towards a social constructionist perspective. *Journal of Contingencies and Crisis Management*, 14 (4), 180–189.

Falkheimer, J., & Heide, M. (2010). Crisis communicators in change: From plans to improvisations. In W. T. Coombs & S. Holladay (Eds), *Handbook of crisis communication* (pp. 511–526). Malden, MA: Wiley-Blackwell.

Falkheimer, J., & Heide, M. (2011a). Inledning: Strategisk kommunikation som forskningsfält och praktik. In J. Falkheimer & M. Heide (Eds), *Strategisk kommunikation: Forskning och praktik*. Lund: Studentlitteratur.

Falkheimer, J., & Heide, M. (Eds). (2011b). *Strategisk kommunikation: Forskning och praktik*. Lund: Studentlitteratur.

Falkheimer, J., & Heide, M. (2012). Participatory pre-crisis and crisis communication: A conceptual approach. In B. A. Olaniran, D. E. Williams & W. T. Coombs (Eds), *Pre-crisis planning, communication, and management: Planning for the inevitable* (pp. 37–56). New York: Peter Lang Publishing.

Falkheimer, J., & Heide, M. (2014). From public relations to strategic communication in sweden: The emergence of a transboundary field of knowledge. *NORDICOM Review*, 35(2), 123–139.

Falkheimer, J., & Heide, M. (2016). A reflexive perspective on public relations: On leaving traditional thinking and uncover the taken-for-granted. In J. L'Etang, D. McKie, N. Snow & J. Xifra (Eds), *The Routledge handbook of critcial public relations* (pp. 162–172). New York: Routledge.

Falkheimer, J., Heide, M., Simonsson, C., Zerfass, A., & Verhoeven, P. (2016). Doing the right things or doing things right?: Paradoxes and Swedish communication professionals' roles and challenges. *Corporate Communications: An International Journal*, 21(2), 142–159.

Falkheimer, J., Heide, M., Nothaft, H., von Platen, S., Simonsson, C., & Andersson, R. (2017). Is strategic communication too important to be left to communication professionals? Managers' and coworkers' attitudes towards strategic communication and communication professionals? *Public Relations Review*, 43(1), 91–101.

Festinger, L. (1957). *A theory of cognitive dissonance*. Stanford, CA: Stanford University Press.

Fink, S. (1986). *Crisis management: Planning for the inevitable*. New York: American Management Association.

Fisher, W. R. (1987). *Human communication as narration: Toward a philosophy of reason, value, and action*. Columbia, SC: University of South Carolina Press.

Fondas, N., & Stewart, R. (1994). Enactment in managerial jobs: A role analysis. *Journal of Management Studies*, 31(1), 83–103.

Ford, J. D., & Ford, L. W. (1995). The role of conversations in producing intentional change in organizations. *Academy of Management Review*, 20(3), 541–571.

Frandsen, F., & Johansen, W. (2017). *Organizational crisis communication*, London: Sage.

Fredriksson, M., & Pallas, J. (2013). *Med synlighet som ledstjärna: En analys av vilka principer som styr kommunikationsarbetet i nationella förvaltningsmyndigheter*. Uppsala: Department of Informatics and Media, Uppsala University.

Freeman, R. E. (1984). *Strategic management: A stakeholder approach*. Boston, MA: Pitman.

Fromm, E. (1978). *To have or to be?* London: Cape.

Fuchs , C. (2013). Social media and capitalism. In T. Olsson (Ed.), *Producing the internet: Critical perspectives of social media*. Gothenburg, Sweden: Nordicom.

Gadamer, H.-G. (1989). *Truth and method*. London: Sheed & Ward.

Galtung, J., & Ruge, M. H. (1965). The structure of foreign news. *Journal of Peace Research*, 2, 64–90.

Gans, H. (1979). *Deciding what's news: A study of CBS evening news, NBC nightly news, Newsweek, and Time*. New York: Pantheon Books.

Geertz, C. (1973). *The interpretation of cultures*. New York: Basic Books.

Gergen, K. J. (1999). *An invitation to social construction*. London: Sage.

Giddens, A. (1990). *The consequences of modernity*. Cambridge: Polity.

Gilpin, D. R., & Murphy, P. J. (2006). Reframing crisis management through complexity. In C. H. Botan & V. Hazleton (Eds), *Public relations theory II* (pp. 375–392). Mahwah, NJ: Lawrence Erlbaum.

Global Alliance. (2010). Stockholm accords: Final text. Retrieved 2016-04-20 from www.stockholmaccords.org/accords-text

Goffman, E. (1959). *The presentation of self in everyday life*. New York: Doubleday.

Goldhaber, G. M. (1993). *Organizational communication* (6th edn). Madison, WI: Brown & Benchmark.

Goodman, M. B. (2000). Corporate communication: The American picture. *Corporate Communications: An International Journal*, 5(2), 69–74.

Gregory, A. (2008). Competencies of senior communication practitioners in the UK: An initial study. *Public Relations Review*, 34(3), 215–223.

Gregory, A., & Willis, P. (2013). *Strategic public relations leadership*. London: Routledge.

Grönroos, C. (1994). From marketing mix to relationship marketing: Towards a paradigm shift in marketing. *Management Decision*, 32(2), 4–20.

Grönroos, C. (2000). *Service management and marketing: A customer relationship management approach*. Chichester: John Wiley & Sons.

Grönroos, C. (2012). Conceptualising value co-creation: A journey to the 1970s and back to the future. *Journal of Marketing Management*, 28(13/14), 1520–1534.

Grönroos, C. (2015). *Service management and marketing: Managing the service profit logic*. Chichester: John Wiley & Sons. Grunig, J. E. (1992). Communication, public relations, and effective organizations: An overview of the book. In J. E. Grunig (Ed.), *Excellence in public relations and communication management* (pp. 1–28). Hillsdale, NJ: Lawrence Erlbaum.

Grunig, J. E. (1997). A situational theory of publics: Conceptual history, recent challenges and new research. In D. Moss, T. MacManus & D. Veric (Eds), *Public relations research: An international perspective* (pp. 3–46). London: International Thomson Business Press.

Grunig, J. E. (2001). Two-way symmetrical public relations. In L. Heath Robert (Ed.), *Handbook of public relations* (pp. 11–30). Thousand Oaks, CA: Sage.

Grunig, J. E. (2009). Paradigms of global public relations in an age of digitalisation. *PRism*, 2(9).

Grunig, J. E., Grunig, L. A., & Dozier, D. M. (2006). The excellence theory. In C. H. Botan & V. Hazleton (Eds.), *Public relations theory II* (pp. 21–62). Mahwah, NJ: Lawrence Erlbaum.

Grunig, J. E., & Hunt, T. (1984). *Managing public relations*. Orlando, FL: Harcourt Brace Jovanovich.

Grunig, J. E., & Repper, F. C. (1992). Strategic management, publics, and issues. In J. E. Grunig (Ed.), *Excellence in public relations and communication management* (pp. 117–158). Hillsdale, NJ: Lawrence Erlbaum Associates.

Grunig, L. A., Grunig, J. E., & Dozier, D. M. (2002). *Excellent public relations and effective organizations: A study of communication management in three countries*. Mahwah, NJ: Lawrence Erlbaum.

Gummesson, E. (1995). Relationship marketing: Its role in the service. In W. J. Glynn & J. G. Barnes (Eds), *Understanding service management* (pp. 244–268). New York: John Wiley & Sons.

Gustafsson, A., Kristensson, P., & Witell, L. (2012). Customer co-creation in service innovation: A matter of communication? *Journal of Service Management*, 23(3), 311–327.

Habermas, J. (1984). *The theory of communicative action*. London: Polity Press.

Habermas, J. (1989). *The structural transformation of the public sphere: An inquiry into a category of bourgeois society*. Cambridge: Polity Press.

Hall, S. (1978). *Policing the crisis: Mugging, the state, and law and order*. London: Macmillan.

Hallahan, K., Holtzhausen, D., van Ruler, B., Verčič, D., & Sriramesh, K. (2007). Defining strategic communication. *International Journal of Strategic Communication*, 1 (1), 3–35.

Hargie, O., & Tourish, D. (2004). How are we doing? Measuring and monitoring organizational communication. In D. Tourish & O. Hargie (Eds), *Key issues in organizational communication* (pp. 234–251). London: Routledge.

Hatch, M. J., & Schultz, M. (2010). Toward a theory of brand co-creation with implications for brand governance. *Journal of Brand Management*, 17(8), 590–604.

Hayes, A. F., Glynn, C. J., & Shanahan, J. (2005). Willingness to self-censor: A construct and measurement tool for public opinion research. *International Journal of Public Opinion Research*, 17(3), 298–323.

Hearit, K. M. (1999). Newsgroups, activist publics, and corporate apologia: The case of Intel and its Pentium chip. *Public Relations Review*, 3(25), 291–308.

Heath, R. L. (2001). A rhetorical enactment rationale for public relations. In R. L. Heath (Ed.), *Handbook of public relations* (pp. 31–50). Thousand Oaks, CA: Sage.

Heath, R. L. (2010). Introduction. In T. W. Coombs & S. J. Holladay (Eds.), *The handbook of crisis communication* (pp. 1–13). Malden, MA: Wiley-Blackwell.

Heide, M. (2002). *Intranät: En ny arena för kommunikation och lärande* ([Intranet: A new arena for communication and learning]). Lund: Lunds universitet, Sociologiska institutionen.

Heide, M. (2013). Internal crisis communication: The future of crisis communication. In A. Thiessen (Ed.), *Handbook of crisis management*. Berlin: Springer.

Heide, M. (2014). Power (as social construction). In R. L. Heath (Ed.), *Encyclopedia of public relations II*. Thousand Oaks, CA: Sage.

Heide, M., Johansson, C., & Simonsson, C. (2012). *Kommunikation i organisationer*. Malmö: Liber.

Heide, M., & Simonsson, C. (2011). Putting co-workers in the limelight: New challenges for communication professionals. *International Journal of Strategic Communication*, 5(4), 201–220.

Heide, M., & Simonsson, C. (2014). Developing internal crisis communication: New roles and practices of communication professionals. *Corporate Communictaions: An International Journal*, 19(2), 128–146.

Heide, M., & Simonsson, C. (2015). Struggling with internal crisis communication: A balancing act between paradoxical tensions. *Public Relations Inquiry*, 4(2), 223–255.

Heide, M., & Simonsson, C. (2018). Coworkership and engaged communicators: A critical reflection on employee engagement. In K. Johnston & M. Taylor (Eds), *The handbook of communication engagement*. Malden, MA: Wiley-Blackwell.

Heider, F. (1958). *The psychology of interpersonal relations*. New York: Wiley.

Heron, A. R. (1942). *Sharing information with employees*. Palo Alto, CA: Stanford University Press.

Holtzhausen, D. R. (2002). Towards a postmodern research agenda for public relations. *Public Relations Review*, 28(3), 251–264.

Holtzhausen, D. R. (2012). *Public relations as activism: Postmodern approaches to theory and practice*. New York: Routledge.

Huber, G. P., & Daft, R. L. (1987). The information environments of organizations. In F. M. Jablin, L. L. Putnam, K. H. Roberts & L. W. Porter (Eds), *Handbook of organizational communication: An interdisciplinary perspective* (pp. 130–164). Newbury Park, CA: Sage.

Hübner, H. (2007). *The communicating organization: Towards an alternative theory of corporate communication*. Heidelberg: Physica Verlag.

Hughes, M. (2011). Do 70 per cent of all organizational change initiatives really fail? *Journal of Change Management*, 11(4), 451–464.

Hutton, J. G. (2001). Defining the relationship between public relations and marketing: Public relation's most important challenge. In R. L. Heath (Ed.), *The handbook of public relations* (pp. 205–214). Thousand Oaks, CA: Sage.

Ihlen, Ø., & Verhoeven, P. (2012). A public relations identity for the 2010s. *Public Relations Inquiry*, 1(2), 159–176.

Ihlen, Ø., Fredrikson, M., & Ruler, B. (2009). *Public relations and social theory: Key figures and concepts*. London: Routledge.

Isaacs, W. N. (1999). *Dialogue and the art of thinking together: A pioneering approach to communicating in business and in life*. London: Currency.

Iyengar, S. (1991). *Is anyone responsible? How television frames political issues*. Chicago, IL: University of Chicago Press.

Jaffe, J. (2007). *Join the conversation: How to engage marketing-weary consumers with the power of community, dialogue, and partnership*. Hoboken, NJ: John Wiley & Sons.

Jansson, A. (2009). *Kommunikation*. Malmö: Liber.

Jarzabkowski, P. (2004). Strategy as practice: Recursiveness, adaptation, and practices-in-use. *Organization Studies*, 25(4), 529–560.

Jarzabkowski, P., Balogun, J., & Seidl, D. (2007). Strategizing: The challenges of a practice perspective. *Human Relations*, 60(1), 5–27.

Jarzabkowski, P., & Whittington, R. (2008a). Hard to disagree, mostly. *Strategic Organization*, 6(1), 101–106.

Jarzabkowski, P., & Whittington, R. (2008b). A strategy-as-practice approach to strategy research and education. *Journal of Management Inquiry*, 17(4), 282–286.

Jenkins, H. (2006). *Convergence culture: Where old and new media collide*. New York: New York University Press.

Jensen, I. (2001). Offentlighedsanalyser i public relations. In M. Femö Nielsen (Ed.), *Profil og offentlighed: Public relations for viderekomne*. Frederiksberg: Samfundslitteratur.

Jian, G. W. (2011). Articulating circumstance, identity and practice: Toward a discursive framework of organizational changing. *Organization*, 18(1), 45–64.

Jöever, M. (Ed.). (1985). *Informationens möjligheter*. Malmö: Liber.

Johansson, C., & Heide, M. (2008). Speaking of change: Three communication approaches in studies of organizational change. *Corporate Communications: An International Journal*, 13(3), 288–305.

Johnson, G., Melin, L., & Whittington, R. (2003). Micro strategy and strategizing: Towards an activity-based view. *Journal of Management Studies*, 40(1), 3–22.

Kalla, H. K. (2005). Integrated internal communications: A multidisciplinary perspective. *Corporate Communications: An International Journal*, 10(4), 302–314.

Karmark, E. (2005). Living the brand. In M. Schultz, Y. M. Antorini & F. F. Csaba (Eds.), *Corporate branding: Purpose/people/process* (pp. 103–124). Fredriksberg: Copenhagen Business School Press.

Katz, E., & Lazarsfeld, P. F. (1955). *Personal influence: The part played by people in the flow of mass communications*. Glencoe, IL: Free Press.

Kennan, W. R., & Hazleton, V. (2006). Internal public relations, social capital, and the role of effective organizational communication. In C. H. Botan & V. Hazleton (Eds.), *Public relations theory II* (pp. 311–338). Mahwah, NJ: Lawrence Erlbaum.

Kim, S. Y., & Reber, B. H. (2009). How public relations professionalism influences corporate social responsibility: A survey of practitioners. *Journalism & Mass Communication Quarterly*, 86(1), 157–174.

Kinnick, K. N., & Cameron, G. T. (1994). Teaching public relations management: The current state of the art. *Public Relations Review*, 20(1), 69–84.

Kliatchko, J. (2009). IMC 20 years after: A second look at IMC definitions. *International Journal of Integrated Marketing Communications*, 1(2), 7–12.

Knights, D., & Morgan, G. (1991). Corporate strategy, organizations, and subjectivity: A critique. *Organization Studies*, 12(2), 251–273.

Kotler, P., Kevin Lane. (2016). *Marketing management* (15th edn). Harlow: Pearson.

Kotter, J. P. (1996). *Leading change*. Harvard, MA: Harvard Business School Press.

Kotter, J. P., & Schlesinger, L. A. (2008). Choosing strategies for change. *Harvard Business Review*, 86(7/8), 130–142.

L'Etang, J. (2004a). Critical public relations: Some reflections. *Public Relations Review*, 31(4), 521–526.

L'Etang, J. (2004b). *Public relations in Britain: A history of the professional practice in the 20th century*. Mahwah, NJ: Lawrence Erlbaum.

L'Etang, J., & Pieczka, M. (Eds). (1996). *Critical perspectives in public relations*. London: International Thomson Business Press.

Larsson, L. (2005). *Upplysning och propaganda. Utvecklingen av svensk PR och information*. Lund: Studentlitteratur.

Lasswell, H. D. (1948). The structure and function of communication in society. In L. Bryson (Ed.), *The communication of ideas*. New York: Harper.

Lavidge, R. J., & Steiner, G. A. (1961). A model for predictive measurements of advertising effectiveness. *Journal of Marketing*, 25(October), 59–62.

Lazarsfeld, P. F., Gaudet, H. F., & Berelson, B. (1968). *The people's choice: How the voter makes up his mind in a presidential campaign*. New York: Columbia University Press.

Leonardi, P. M., & Bailey, D. E. (2008). Transformational technologies and the creation of new work practices: Making implicit knowledge explicit in task-based offshoring. *Mis Quarterly*, 32(2), 411–436.

Lerbinger, O. (1997). *The crisis manager: Facing risk and responsibility*. Mahwah, NJ: Lawrence Erlbaum.

Lesley, U. (2004). *Integrerad kommunikation – i praktiken*. Malmö: Liber.

Levitt, T. (1981). Marketing intangible products and product intangibles. *Harvard Business Review*, 59(3), 94–103.

Lewin, K. (1951). *Field theory in social science: Selected theoretical papers*. New York: Harper & Row.

Lewis, L. K. (2011). *Organizational change: Creating change through strategic communication*. Chichester: Wiley-Blackwell.

Lewis, L. K. (2014). Organizational change and innovation. In L. L. Putnam & D. K. Mumby (Eds), *The new handbook of organizational communication* (pp. 503–524). Thousand Oaks, CA: Sage.

Lindenmann, W. K. (1993). An 'effectiveness yardstick' to measure public relations success. *Public Relations Quarterly*, 38(1), 7–9.

Lippman, W. (1922/1997). *Public opinion*. New York: Free Press.

Lull, J. (2007). *Culture-on-demand: Communication in a crisis world*. Malden, MA: Blackwell.

Lund, A. K., & Petersen, H. (2002). *De 12 bud: Danske topledere om kommunikation*. Fredrksberg: Samfundslitteratur.

Lyotard, J.-F. (1996). The postmodern condition: A report on knowledge. In L. Cahoone (Ed.), *From modernism to postmodernism: An anthology*. Oxford: Blackwell.

Macnamara, J. (2015). *Creating an 'architecture of listening' in organizations: The basis of engagement, trust, healthy democracy, social equity, and business sustainability*. Sydney, NSW: University of Technology Sydney.

Maitlis, S., & Christianson, M. (2014). Sensemaking in organizations: Taking stock and moving forward. *Academy of Management Annals*, 8(1), 57–125.

Maitlis, S., & Sonenshein, S. (2010). Sensemaking in crisis and change: Inspiration and insights from Weick (1988). *Journal of Management Studies*, 47(3), 551–580.

Manning, P. (2001). *News and news sources: A critical introduction*. London: Sage.

Marchiori, M., & Bulgacov, S. (2012). Strategy as communicational practice in organizations. *International Journal of Strategic Communication*, 6(3), 199–211.

McCombs, M., & Shaw, D. (1972). The agenda-setting function of mass media. *Public Opinion Quarterly*, 36(2), 176–187.

McKie, D. (2001). Updating public relations: "New science", research paradigms, and uneven developments. In R. L. Heath (Ed.), *Handbook of public relations* (pp. 75–91). Thousand Oaks, CA: Sage.

McQuail, D. (2010). *McQuail's mass communication theory* (6th edn). London: Sage.

Mintzberg, H. (1973). Strategy-making in three modes. *California Management Review*, 16(2), 44–53.

Mintzberg, H., & Lampel, J. (1999). Reflecting on the strategy process. *Sloan Management Review*, 40(3), 21–30.

Mintzberg, H., & Westley, F. (2001). Decision making: It's not what you think. *MIT Sloan Management Review*, 42(3), 89–93.

Mitchell, A. (2004). Getting staff to live the brand: Work in process. *Marketing Week*, September 2, 30–31.

Mitroff, I. I., & Anagnos, G. (2001). *Managing crises before they happen: What every executive needs to know about crisis management*. New York: AMACOM.

Moriarty, S. (1997). IMC needs PR's stakeholder focus. *Marketing News*, 31(11), 7.

Morley, D., Shockley-Zalabak, P., & Cesaria, R. (2002). Organizational influence processes: Perceptions of values, communication and effectiveness. *Studies in Communication Sciences*, 2, 69–104.

Moss, D., Newman, A., & DeSanto, B. (2005). What do communication managers do? Defining and refining the core elements of management in a public relations/corporate communication context. *Journalism & Mass Communication Quarterly*, 82(4), 873–890.

Moss, D., Warnaby, G., & Newman, A. J. (2000). Public relations practitioner role enactment at the senior managment level within UK companies. *Journal of Public Relations Research*, 12(4), 277–307.

Moss, D., Warnaby, G., & Thame, L. (1996). Tactical publicity or strategic relationship management? An exploratory investigation of the role of public relations in the UK retail sector. *European Journal of Marketing*, 30(12), 69–84.

Mumby, D. (2011). *Reframing difference in organizational communication studies*. Thousand Oaks, CA: Sage.

Murphy, P. (1996). Chaos theory as a model for managing issues and crises. *Public Relations Review*, 22(2), 95–113.

Nissen, T. E. (2014). Terror.com: IS's social media warfare in Syria and Iraq. *Military Studies Magazine*, 2(1), 2.

Noelle-Neumann, E. (1993). *The spiral of silence*. London: University of Chicago Press.

Normann, R. (1984). *Service management: Strategy and leadership in service business*. Chichester: Wiley.

Nothhaft, H. (2010). Communication management as a second-order management function: Roles and functions of the communication executive – results from a shadowing study. *Journal of Communication Management*, 14(2), 127–140.

Orlikowski, W. J. (1992). The duality of technology: Rethinking the concept of technology in organizations. *Organization Science*, 3(3), 398–427.

Orr, J. E. (1996). *Talking about machines: An ethnography of a modern job*. Ithaca, NY: Cornell University Press.

Pamment, J. (2013). *New public diplomacy in the 21st century: A comparative study of policy and practice*. London: Routledge.

Pavlik, J. V. (1987). *Public relations: What research tells us*. Newbury Park, CA: Sage.

de Pelsmacker, P., Geuens, M., & van den Bergh, J. (2010). *Marketing communications: A European perspective*. Harlow: Prentice Hall.

Peters, T. J. (1992). *Liberation management*. New York: Knopf.

Porter, M. E. (1980). *Competitive strategy: Techniques for analyzing industries and competitors*. New York: The Free Press.

Potter, J., & Wetherell, M. (1987). *Discourse and social psychology: Beyond attitudes and behaviour*. London: Sage.

Powell, W. W., & DiMaggio, P. J. (Eds). (1991). *The new institutionalism in organizational analysis*. Chicago, IL: University of Chicago Press.

Prahalad, C. K., & Ramaswamy, V. (2003). The new frontier of experience innovation. *MIT Sloan Management Review*, 44(4), 12–18.

Prahalad, C. K., & Ramaswamy, V. (2004). Co-creating unique value with customers. *Strategy & Leadership*, 32(3), 4–9.

Proctor, T., & Kitchen, P. (2002). Communication in postmodern integrated marketing. *Corporate Communications: An International Journal*, 7(3), 144–154.

Putnam, L. L., & Nicotera, A. M. (2010). Communicative constitution of organization is a question: Critical issues for addressing it. *Management Communication Quarterly*, 24(1), 158–165.

Putnam, L. L., & Nicotera, A. M. (Eds). (2009). *Building theories of organization*. Thousand Oaks, CA: Sage.

Redding, W. C., & Sanborn, G. A. (1964). *Business and industrial communication: A source book*. New York: Harper & Row.

Reddy, M. J. (1993). The conduit metaphor: A case of frame conflict in our language about language. In A. Ortony (Ed.), *Metaphor and thought* (2nd edn, pp. 164–189). Cambridge, MA: Cambridge University Press.

van Riel, C. B. M. (1995). *Principles of corporate communication*. London: Prentice Hall.

van Riel, C. B. M., & Fombrun, C. J. (2007). *Essentials of corporate communication: Implementing practices for effective reputation management*. London: Routledge.

Rosen, S., & Tesser, A. (1970). On reluctance to communicate undesirable information: The MUM effect. *Sociometry*, 33(3), 253–263.

Rosengren, K. E. (2000). *Communication: An introduction*. London: Sage.

van Ruler, B., & Verčič, D. (Eds). (2004). *Public relations and communication management in Europe: A nation-by-nation introduction to public relations theory and practice*. Berlin: Mouton de Gruyter.

van Ruler, B., & Verčič, D. (2005). Reflective communication management: Future ways for public relations research. *Communication Yearbook 29*, 239–273.

Säljö, R. (1999). Learning as the use of tools: A sociocultural perspective on the human-technology link. In P. Light (Ed.), *Learning with computers: Analysing productive interaction*. London: Routledge.

Santi, N., & Kyoichi, K. (2012). Value co-creation by customer-to-customer communication: Social media and face-to-face for case of airline service selection. *Journal of Service Science and Management*, 5(1), 101–109.

Schatzki, T. R. (2005). The sites of organizations. *Organization Studies*, 26(3), 465–484.

Schon, D. (1973). *Beyond the stable state: Public and private learning in a changing society*. New York: Norton.

Schultz, D. E., Tannenbaum, S. I., & Lauterborn, R. F. (1993). *Integrated marketing communications: Putting it together & making it work*. Chicago, IL: NTC Business Books.

Schultz, M. (2005). A cross-disciplinary perspective on corporate branding. In M. Schultz, Y. M. Antorini, & F. F. Csaba (Eds), *Corporate branding: Purpose/people/process* (pp. 23–55). Frederiksberg: Copenhagen Business School Press.

Schön, D. A. (1983). *The reflective practioner: How professionals think in action*. Aldershot: Ashgate.

Selznick, P. (1957). *Leadership in administration: A sociological interpretation*. New York: Harper & Row.

Semetko, H. A., & Valkenburg, P. M. (2000). Framing European politics: A content analysis of press and television news. *Journal of Communication*, 50(2), 93–109.

Shannon, C. E., & Weaver, W. (1949). *The mathematical theory of communication*. Urbana, IL: University of Illinois.

Shirky, C. (2009). *Here comes everybody: How change happens when people come together*. London: Penguin.

Shockley-Zalabak, P., & Ellis, K. (2000). Perceived organizational effectiveness, job satisfaction, culture, and communication: Challenging the traditional view. *Communication Research Reports*, 17, 375–386.

Shojaie, S., Matin, H. Z., & Barani, G. (2011). Analyzing the infrastructures of organizational silence and ways to get rid of it. *Social and Behavioral Sciences, 30*, 1731–1735.

Shotter, J. (1993). *Conversational realities: Constructing life through language*. London: Sage.

Simon, H. A. (1947). *Administrative behavior: A study of decision-making processes in administrative organization*. New York: Macmillan.

Simonsson, C. (2002). *Den kommunikativa utmaningen* ([The communicative challenge]). Lund: Lunds universitet.

Simonsson, C. (2006). *Nå fram till medarbetarna*. Malmö: Liber.

Smollan, R. K. (2013). Trust in change managers: The role of affect. *Journal of Change Management*, 26(4), 725–747.

Smudde, P. M. (2005). Blogging, ethics and public relations: A proactive and dialogic approach. *Public Relations Quarterly*, 50(3), 34–38.

Søderberg, A.-M., & Vaara, E. (2003). *Merging across borders: People, cultures and politics*. Copenhagen: Copenhagen Business School Press.

Spotts, H. E., Lambert, D. R., & Joyce, M. L. (1998). Marketing déjà vu: The discovery of integrated marketing communications. *Journal of Marketing Education*, 20(3), 210–219.

Starck, K., & Kruckeberg, D. (2001). Public relations and community: A reconstructed theory revisited.InR. L. Heath (Ed.), *Handbook of public relations* (pp. 51–60). Thousand Oaks, CA: Sage.

Stern, E. (1997). Crisis and learning: A conceptual balance sheet. *Journal of Contingencies & Crisis Management*, 5(2), 69–87.

Steyn, B. (2009). The strategic role of public relations is strategic reflection: A South African research stream. *American Behavioral Scientist*, 53(4), 516–532.

Steyn, B., & Niemann, L. (2010). Enterprise strategy: A concept that explicates corporate communication's strategic contribution at the macro-organisational level. *Journal of Communication Management*, 14(2), 106–126.

Strömbäck, J. (2000). *Makt och medier: Samspelet mellan medborgarna, medierna och de politiska makthavarna.* Lund: Studentlitteratur.

Strömbäck, J., & Kiousis, S. (2011). *Political public relations: Principles and applications.* New York: Routledge.

Sutcliffe, K. M. (2001). Organizational environments and organizational information processing. In F. M. Jablin & L. L. Putnam (Eds), *The new handbook of organizational communication: Advances in theory, research, and methods* (pp. 197–230). Thousand Oaks, CA: Sage.

Sutcliffe, K. M. (2011). High reliability organizations (HROs). *Best Practice & Research Clinical Anaesthesiology*, 25(2), 133–144.

Sveiby, K. E. (1994). Towards a knowledge perspective on organisation (dissertation), Stockholm University, Stockholm.

Sveiby, K. E. (1997). *The new organizational wealth: Managing and measuring knowledge-based assets.* San Francisco, CA: Berrett Koehler.

Taylor, M. (2010). Towards a holistic organizational approach to understanding crisis. In W. T. Coombs & S. J. Holladay (Eds.), *The handbook of crisis communication* (pp. 698–704). Malden, MA: Wiley-Blackwell.

Tench, R., Verčič, D., Zerfass, A., Moreno, A., & Verhoeven, P. (2017). *Communication excellence: How to develop, manage and lead exceptional communications.* London: Palgrave Macmillan.

Tench, R., Verhoeven, P., & Zerfass, A. (2009). Institutionalizing strategic communication in Europe – an ideal home or a madhouse? Evidence from a survey in 37 countries. *International Journal of Strategic Communication*, 3(2), 147–164.

Thompson, J. B. (1995). *The media and modernity: A social theory of the media.* Cambridge: Polity.

Timmerman, P. D., & Harrison, W. (2005). The discretionary use of electronic media: Four considerations for bad news bearers. *Journal of Business Communication*, 42(4), 379–389.

Tindall, N. T. J., & Holtzhausen, D. R. (2011). Toward a roles theory for strategic communication: The case of South Africa. *International Journal of Strategic Communication*, 5(2), 74–94.

Torp, S. (2008). Integreret markedskommunikation. In K. Eiberg, E. Karsholt, & S. Torp (Eds), *Integreret markedskommunikation* (pp. 9–18). Fredriksberg: Samfundslitteratur.

Toth, E. L. (2002). Postmodernism for modernist public relations: The cash value and application of critical research in public relations. *Public Relations Review*, 28(3), 243–250.

Toth, E. L., Serini, S. A., Wright, D. K., & Emig, A. G. (1998). Trends in public relations: 1990–1995. *Public Relations Review*, 24(2), 145–163.

Tourish, D., & Hargie, O. (2004a). The communication consequences of downsizing trust, loyalty and commitment. In D. Tourish & O. Hargie (Eds), *Key issues in organizational communication* (pp. 17–36). London: Routledge.

Tourish, D., & Hargie, O. (2004b). Motivating critical upward communication: A key challenge for management decision making. In D. Tourish & O. Hargie (Eds), *Key issues in organizational communication* (pp. 188–204). London: Routledge.

Tsai, S.-P. (2005). Integrated marketing as management of holistic consumer experience. *Business Horizons*, 48(5), 431–441.

Tyler, L. (2005). Towards a postmodern understanding of crisis communication. *Public Relations Review*, 31(4), 566–571.

Ulmer, R. R., Sellnow, T. L., & Seeger, M. W. (2007). *Effective crisis communication: Moving from crisis to opportunity*. Thousand Oaks, CA: Sage.

Ulrich, D., & Brockbank, W. (2005). *The HR value proposition*. Boston, MA: Harvard Business School.

Ulrich, D., Younger, J., Brockbank, W., & Ulrich, M. D. (2013). The state of the HR profession. *Human Resource Management*, 52(3), 457–471.

Uzunoğlu, E., & Misci Kip, S. (2014). Brand communication through digital influencers: Leveraging blogger engagement. *International Journal of Information Management*, 34(5), 592–602.

Varey, R. J. (2000). A critical review of conceptions of communication evident in contemporary business and management literature. *Journal of Communication Management*, 4(4), 328–340.

Vargo, S. L. (2011). Market systems, stakeholders and value propositions: Toward a service-dominant logic-based theory of the market. *European Journal of Marketing*, 45 (1/2), 217–222.

Vargo, S. L., & Lusch, R. F. (2004). Evolving to a new dominant logic for marketing. *Journal of Marketing*, 68(1), 1–17.

Vargo, S. L., & Lusch, R. F. (2015). Institutions and axioms: An extension and update of service-dominant logic. *Journal of the Academy of Marketing Science*, 44(1), 5–23.

Verčič, D., van Ruler, B., & Flodin, B. (2001). On the definition of public relations: A European view. *Public Relations Review*, 27(4), 373–387.

Verhoeven, P., Zerfass, A., & Tench, R. (2011). Strategic orientation of communication professionals in Europe. *International Journal of Strategic Communication*, 5(2), 95–117.

Vygotsky, L. S. (1978). *Mind in society: The development of higher psychological processes*. Cambridge, MA: Harvard University Press.

Earl, S. & Waddington, S. (2012). *Brand anarchy*. London: Bloomsbury.

Wehmeier, S., & Winkler, P. (2013). Expanding the bridge, minimizing the gaps: Public relations, organizational communication, and the idea that communication constitutes organization. *Management Communication Quarterly*, 27(2), 280–290.

Weick, K. E. (1979). *The social psychology of organizing* (2nd edn). Reading, MA: Addison-Wesley.

Weick, K. E. (1988). Enacted sensemaking in crisis situations. *Journal of Management Studies*, 25(4), 305–317.

Weick, K. E. (1990). The vulnerable system: An analysis of the Tenerife air disaster. *Journal of Management*, 16(3), 571–593.

Weick, K. E. (1993). The collapse of sensemaking in organizations: The Mann Gulch disaster. *Administrative Science Quarterly*, 38(4), 628–652.

Weick, K. E. (1995). *Sensemaking in organizations*. Thousand Oaks, CA: Sage.

Weick, K. E. (1998). Improvisation as a mindset for organizational analysis. *Organization Science: A Journal of the Institute of Management Sciences*, 9(5), 543–556.

Weick, K. E. (2001). *Making sense of the organization*. Oxford: Blackwell Business.

Weick, K. E. (2004). A bias for conversation: Acting discursively in organizations. In D. Grant, C. Hardy, C. Oswick, & L. Putnam (Eds), *The Sage handbook of organizational discourse* (pp. 405–412). London: Sage.

Weick, K. E. (2015). Ambiguity as grasp: The reworking of sense. *Journal of Contingencies and Crisis Management*, 23(2), 117–123.

Weick, K. E., Sutcliffe, K. M., & Obstfeld, D. (2005). Organizing and the process of sensemaking. *Organization Science*, 16(4), 409–422.

Werder, K. P., & Holtzhausen, D. (2011). Organizational structures and their relationship with communication management practices: A public relations perspective from the United States. *International Journal of Strategic Communication*, 5(2), 118–142.

White, C., & Park, J. (2010). Public perceptions of public relations. *Public Relations Review*, 36(4), 319–324.

Whittington, R. (2001). *What is strategy and does it matter?* London: Thomson Learning.

Whittington, R. (2004). Strategy after modernism: Recovering practice. *European Management Review*, 1, 62–68.

Whittington, R. (2006). Completing the practice turn in strategy research. *Organization Studies*, 27(5), 613–634.

Whittington, R. (2007). Strategy practice and strategy process: Family differences and the sociological eye. *Organization Studies*, 28(10), 1575–1586.

Whitworth, B. (2006). Internal communication. In T. L. Gillis (Ed.), *The IABC handbook of organizational communication: A guide to internal communication, public relations, marketing, and leadership* (pp. 205–214). San Francisco, CA: Jossey-Bass.

Wilson, D. C., & Jarzabkowski, P. (2004). Thinking and acting strategically: New challenges for interrogating strategy. *European Management Review*, 1(1), 14–20.

Wilson, L. (2000). *Strategic program planning for effective public relations campaign.* Dubuque, IA: Kendall/Hunt.

Windahl, S., & Signitzer, B. (2009). *Using communication theory: An introduction to planned communication* (2nd edn). London: Sage.

Zerfass, A., & Franke, N. (2013). Enabling, advising, supporting, executing: A theoretical framework for internal communication consulting within organizations. *International Journal of Strategic Communication*, 7(2), 118–135.

Zerfass, A., & Huck, S. (2007). Innovation, communication, and leadership: New developments in strategic communication. *International Journal of Strategic Communication*, 1(2), 107–122.

Zerfass, A., Tench, R., Verčič, D., Verhoeven, P., & Moreno, A. (2017). *European communication monitor 2017. Excellence in strategic communication: How strategic communication deals with the challenges of visualisation, social bots and hypermodernity. Results of a survey in 50 countries.* Brussels: EACD/EUPRERA, Quadriga Media Berlin.

Index